# The Naive Woman And Mother

# The Naive Woman And Mother

*Love, Children, Money & the Incorporation*

Tricia Rintoul

Copyright © 2010 by Tricia Rintoul.

| | | |
|---|---|---|
| Library of Congress Control Number: | | 2010917117 |
| ISBN: | Hardcover | 978-1-4568-1855-5 |
| | Softcover | 978-1-4568-1854-8 |
| | Ebook | 978-1-4568-1856-2 |

All rights reserved. No part of this book may be reproduced or transmitted in any form or by any means, electronic or mechanical, including photocopying, recording, or by any information storage and retrieval system, without permission in writing from the copyright owner.

This book was printed in the United States of America.

**To order additional copies of this book, contact:**
Xlibris Corporation
1-888-795-4274
www.Xlibris.com
Orders@Xlibris.com
87408

# CONTENTS

Prologue ........................................................................................... 9

| Chapter 1 | A New Man in My Life ............................................ 15 |
| Chapter 2 | The Courtship ........................................................ 22 |
| Chapter 3 | The Marriage ......................................................... 26 |
| Chapter 4 | The Children/Grandchildren ................................. 35 |
| Chapter 5 | Good Times ........................................................... 46 |
| Chapter 6 | The Secret Shame .................................................. 50 |
| Chapter 7 | The Assault ............................................................ 58 |
| Chapter 8 | My Family .............................................................. 62 |
| Chapter 9 | The Craziest Divorce Ever ..................................... 66 |
| Chapter 10 | The Incorporation .................................................. 71 |
| Chapter 11 | The Destruction of a Family .................................. 73 |
| Chapter 12 | The Importance of Wonderful Old Friends, Cohorts, New Friends and Achievements ............ 77 |
| Chapter 13 | Empowerment, Education and Forgetting ........... 82 |

Epilogue ......................................................................................... 85

# Dedication

Dedicated to all the hundreds of wives that are honest, trusting, unsuspecting, and are financially naive. My hope is they may be inspired to improve their judgement after reading my story, and it will help me to gain insight and relinquish my pain.

I work every day to put behind me and to try to find a place of happiness in my friends to not let my husband and kids rob me of my self-worth of happiness in my future.

Maybe I can make a difference for others. Divorce is traumatic enough without the distress of the unknown—children, money and the Incorporation.

# PROLOGUE

I knew that May 7, 2004 would change my life, but it would not change me and my principles and values.

I woke up at 9:00 a.m. that day, as I had always done on Saturday mornings. The routine since we built the cottage 17 years ago, was for my husband and I to go to the cottage after a week of long days work in the city. Sometimes we drove on our own depending on time. Saturday morning then began with a coffee and a muffin. I savoured that first coffee. I said "Good Morning" to my husband and alluded to a comment he made on our way home from friends after playing cards the night before. It was also about a repetitious comment that had been hurdled at me for sometime over the past year. "Just wait until your elder daughter gets you." My concerns had become more urgent and researching since I retired in December 2003 attempting to understand our financials. I discovered they were not forthcoming and Tom had become exceedingly irritated with me using more verbal abusive language and two incidents of physical violence. I had sat down with him in November 2004 suggesting his anger rages were new to me and becoming out of control and I would not tolerate another outburst and he should think about Anger Management.

As I sat in the chair in my bedtime attire I knew that Tom was anxious while reading his many reports which he did regularly in the morning while sitting at this long Board Room table he had acquired from a Northern Company. Within moments, after the question about Carey, he had repeatedly stated for months when he was in a bad mood, "Wait until your daughter gets you." Tom exploded irrationally, throwing his reports all over the room, jumped the table and he had me by the neck repeatedly saying "You do not understand" while I struggled and pleaded to let go. In such a state,

I validated all his verbiage, while he sparked hatred and rage and I finally got loose in order to run to my bedroom, lock the door as he attempted to break it down, get dressed and run for my life to the car while gathering up my clothes that had been thrown out on the front deck. I grabbed the dog and drove off in a state of shock.

My prayers were with me as I survived and my thoughts were Tom needs to find himself again. He had been suffering from anxiety and panic attacks and I had visited his physician to have an explanation with no success. The only way would be to get involuntary help through the legal system because we had discussed help for his anger with no results. I had even mentioned to the children and what it does to a family with his ugly moods. They did not seem to be concerned. I had also had a consult with a friend of mine over the last year about this behaviour. She was a social worker and told me if it happened again to use the legal system to get Tom help. These rages only escalated causing serious trauma.

I was driving to the police office to report the incident that a lawyer assured me would get "Anger Management" help for my husband.

The cell phone rang "How are you?" Carey, my youngest daughter, questioned. "How am I? How do you think I am?" "I was just assaulted, thrown out and called a gutless woman by your father."

"Do you know what you are doing?" she said in an excited tone and I said "Yes, and it is the only way your father will get help." His anger is completely out of control and he will hurt someone if not managed."

The cell phone rang again. "How are you? Are you okay?" It was my young brother of whom I did not realize would know about the incident.

I was in a surreal situation that my thought process was completely void except I knew in my heart that Tom needed help for a long time as he escalated his abusive and arrogant behaviour and I must take the lead. He had also threatened my life when he would be returning to the city later the same day. I related this to my brother.
There had been many moments over the past months and probably years that found myself crying, but I realized this was not one of them. I must try

to keep myself level-headed and get this man help while protecting myself and family.

The police were kind and understanding and I answered all their questions as they questioned his irrational behaviour, and guns in the house. They stated that I had acted accordingly to validate his remarks and quickly removed myself as there were guns in the house. Very important for them to know. They were under his bed.

As a volunteer Board member of a centre for battered wives, I still stand that no man has the right to physically attack a woman and especially his wife. The ride to the city was a fog. His attitude had to change and my children had to take it seriously.

What the future held was something I, the newly-retired professional woman looking for peace and travel, could not imagine I had asked Tom in one of his more lucid moments about plans. Would he travel now even to visit my friend in Ireland and he said "Yes." Could I imagine a life without Tom, the man whose ambitions had been the centre of our family right from day one starting 40 years ago. Without him, what were my directions. Kids had grown and I had five grandchildren. I had already some life-changing decisions with retirement, with volunteering and the love of Bridge. Maybe this would sort itself out but I still had two grown children and their families for support and to assist Tom to get his emotions under control. That was the main goal, I thought.

When I returned to the city family home, I found a message from my sister-in-law and a nursing classmate with some comforting thoughts on the phone. Distance was a fact but she did embrace me with her kindness. In our carefree days we had lots of fun with getting our kids together, etc. This was before the high stress of work and politics. Our kids were cousins and became good friends. I was grateful for her steady support not realizing there was much more to come. My other lifetime friends were very constant as they were when Tom was away so much: Mexico, South America, Northern Canada, etc. What I would not give if my wonderful parents were here to talk to.

It was ten days later, May 17, that a divorce decree was delivered to my door which obviously suggested there was no insight or remorse on the part of Tom. He had also denied the physical assault and persuaded the kids that I was the major problem and they supported him accordingly. At this point, I was in so much shock, it felt as though this was happening to someone else but I had no idea of the money involved in the Incorporation or changes made without legal protocol.

This divorce decree was a mixture of sadness and relief. I knew there would be endless days in interrogation and court appearances as the family lawyer eluded to but I needed financial understanding and independence at the very vulnerable part of my life.

I made my first visit to the lawyer without my children's support which he stated was extremely strange as a practitioner with years of experience that my kids were not there but he had no idea about money and the Incorporation.

What was my relationship with my two daughters and their families to date? There were no negatives and, in fact, good in my mind, I thought I had built integrity, caring, love and honesty in my children. He said daughters are always devoted to a caring mother. She brought you into this world and should be trustworthy and never lie to your mother. I quoted my birthday log which covered my parenting and life with kids. The first lawyer after several attempts to have financial disclosure was unsuccessful because of the changes to the company of which I was not aware and it cost $40,000. A fee many women would find insurmountable. Money becomes essential to a woman to fight for her rights in a divorce.

I knew in my heart and soul from that moment on, husband and kids or not, this time of personal crisis would begin a new time in my life and I needed financial security—retired, and no cheque—a fixed income. I started to nurture more time with my brother, sister-in-law, nursing classmates and great friends realizing this is a late time in life to attempt opening new doors to friendship. I believe that I loved my husband and kids but not their behaviour and have put forth every effort to be a good wife, mother and grandmother for the past 40 years of marriage and parenting. As well, for these last 40 years my husband has been fully employed in a cyclical industry, and I supported him to the best of my ability moving in the first years to seven different houses in nine years and unable to resume my professional work until I had stability in my life.

I believe the greatest legacy I can leave is not the job I held in nursing or the many programs and services I created for a needy community or even the many functions I entertained to enhance Tom's monetary goals. Instead, it is that of a good mother to be proud of honest children while making the world a better place with these positive character values and principles, a passion for their chosen careers, integrity and a love for their children that will see them grow up and build an even better society. At this time in my life because the recent actions of my husband and kids' support, trust and honesty have disseminated. Reality left me with a necessity for treatment for post traumatic shock and my physician was a jewel.

I have always believed about the Institution of Marriage as a companionship, sharing for growth, connecting and most of all, trust, which I consistently attempted in my actions but as time moved on with the assault and divorce proceedings discovered I had lived with a man of deceit and conned my children to signature falsifying documents of minutes of the so-called family company. When I found out about my husband's omission and fraudulent intent to cheat me inclusive of children about his two companies and heaven-knows maybe other things, I felt I must hold onto my dignity, self-respect and my basic sense of right or wrong and fight the fight I never knew I had the strength to do. I therefore hired another lawyer to assure my security in my retirement life. A lawyer that knew my accomplishments to society and would represent me with the best-ever skills. He had semi-retired but came to my rescue. He had volunteered in community services for years as a great man to help the oppressed and I had worked with him. He had a heart of gold and had demonstrated a brilliant mind for Family Law. The first and most important goal was to obtain a financial worth of my husband to obtain equalization. The process was legally facilitated by lawyers which became an impossible as Tom submitted only partial and small amounts because he had all the money in the companies that he had successfully frozen with the help of my daughters who at the time were Directors. It was also made easy to use his money with me paying for food, clothing, furniture, car payments. (See Estate Freeze references.)

I believed that love and marriage was primarily a commitment and act of honesty, trust and loyalty but it must be reciprocal and as evidence came out from companies and minutes and motions belief in Tom and my kids became nil. The sad part is I thought I raised honourable children and even after it is all done there was no true spirit of humility or remorse.

This has been a very painful time for me realizing I was so naive about a man I lived with 40 years and children I thought I had raised with honesty and a great empathy but they ended up committing financial elder abuse, supporting falsifying records and fraud. I had to lean heavy on God and friends during this terrible time.

# CHAPTER 1

## A New Man in My Life

I drove the unfamiliar roads to the Unico Company in Sandy Lake country. I wondered why I was making this bumpy road trip to see Tom. It was 1959, and I had only been on the phone to this man and a weekend joint date in my home town. The double date was with a friend, Molly and her love-at-first sight, Wally, another engineer. These trips from my home town to Sandy Lake went on for a few months with other couples joining us—not exactly a recipe for a romance. Shortly thereafter, Tom invited me to spend Thanksgiving at his parents' home in Springtown. I found the invite interesting because Tom was not like other men I had dated. He seemed overly ambitious in his career plans and showed no interest in settling down. I asked my Mom what she thought "Nothing to lose, he seems like a fun guy," she said. "Go and meet his family, and it will give you a better perspective." I agreed with her as life is a series of experiences and I should challenge something new. He also was easy on the eyes and sometimes unquestionably charming. Mom would later on say, "He sure had us fooled."

It was an interesting drive in his little old Volkswagen. When I had just graduated from Nursing, I had purchased a Volkswagen and found the stick shift impossible so traded in on a Ford in which many of my friends and I had great fun. All these years, I remember the night we three nurses had a flat tire and attempted to change the tire until a very kind man came to our assistance. We had no flashlights just a match or two.
I had first met Tom in Michigan, U.S.A. about six months earlier, on an evening at a bar—the El Mar, a hang-out for many singles. My friends Molly and Ilene had decided we needed a night out. We women were not

drinkers but nursed a Coke for a night while enjoying the dancing and music. I was the driver that dispatched us to this outing using my brother's '44 Chevrolet. When we were ready to leave, Tom asked us if he could catch a ride in this beat-up old car and we agreed. We all packed in with Tom's tall, very lanky frame leaving us very tight and beer flatulence almost unbearable. "Open up the windows," someone said.

There was something very attractive about Tom from the start with his light wit about life. As an example, he was kidding around that he had forgotten where he was staying as he lived 90 miles out of the city. However, he could also be very sarcastic that did not get approval of my friends. We exchanged phone numbers but I recall it was only a passing fancy as I was involved with another man. We were all young—I was 24 and something long-term was still really not in my radar yet, more education and experience were. I loved nursing, excitement, emergencies and a great feeling of outcomes.

As we journeyed along to Springtown, there was a connection that took us to defining our own individual goals. It was very engaging as two professionals that reached a certain hype. He spoke of his family with his negative sense of humour. Two sisters, one married with a husband Greg and a child James, the other in her teens. His two brothers were married both working for a bank. No kids as yet.

We arrived in good time to be welcomed warmly by his mother Rosie and father Edgar, who had the same negative sense of humour. "Can you paint a room?" said he. "If you can't, don't expect to marry into this family." My mind instantly thought "and who said I want to." I think paint was on his mind as a landlord and many rentals.

His sister Nelly appeared from the kitchen and greeted me. She directed me to a chair at the large table as we had arrived in time for dinner. There were many questions but not the kind of familial gathering I was accustomed to having with my family—laughing, connecting and enjoying good company. After finishing a delicious dinner, we sat comfortably and Edgar, Tom's father, suggested we would have time to see the cottage tomorrow.

As I fell asleep that night in a small but comfy bedroom, I felt I had passed a test and thought why do I want to get a pass. There certainly was a lot I did not know about him or his family.

Tom was an engineer working at a small company and had graduated in 1958 and I could tell was as highly driven as was his father. Status, money and credentials were very important. His ambitions were of some interest but my life goals were to do what you were passionate about and keep life in balance.

Love was more than a feeling or emotion to me. It was a give and take with empathy on a daily basis. I had a serious relationship in Nursing School but my mother said it was an infatuation and she was right as it did not last and the feeling faded after I visited him in Montreal. I also had a few brief relationships as the one I was in at this time but could not take serious or to a higher level. Curt was the present relationship I was in, an engineer as well, but was on a three month assignment in Winnipeg. My date at graduation was a lawyer from Toronto and a real card but I never got the feeling for a further relationship but maybe should have in retrospect. A devoted Catholic and son to his wonderful Mom. His brother was his advocate and thought we were so meant for each other.

Tom's ambitions were of some intrigue to me but his high living life of drinking and racing his car and several times having accidents (turning over twice and totalling the car) put me on hold but the sparks were starting to fly after about nine months of courtship, which was part of my appeal for this man. Getting to know each other seemed hard as he never really would open his heart. I had witnessed my parents' complete declaration to each other and the feeling of security and stability it had given to me as I grew up. They were both steady and open to any dialogue—a complete feeling of being loved, cared for and stable.

My paternal grandmother had lost her husband early in her life but remained loyal in love with Herbert until she died. I would visit her home every day on my way home from school and we would visit his picture. She led by good example as there was no welfare in those days but she made her home into a Boarding House enjoying every new people that came to stay to work until they were more successful. It provided income and socialization. She taught me to get into work young in life—babysitting or whatever.

I had envisioned my life a career and a love in my life taking the same road if I committed to a man that would inspire that kind of life that would involve understanding values, standards and goals. I knew from my parents that passion, sex and intimacy come and go but a solid empathy would be the glue to hold the relationship together.

As I awoke, Tom came to tell me breakfast was served and the trip to the cottage would follow. As I slipped into my attire, I could smell the aroma of bacon and eggs from the kitchen. His father was cooking as he did often. The daylight grew brighter as Tom held my hand and led me to his father's car awaiting the journey to the cottage on Ball Lake in a collaboration of small lakes. The ride was interesting as we drove down a rather winding road, up and down hills and being interrogated by Tom's father. Another test while be bragged intermittently about his Cadillac and status of important people that he interfaced with at his home in Florida and his retirement suggesting wealth. At times, I felt uncomfortable with this overbearing and somewhat arrogant stance to his life not family.

As we drove, I became aware of the beauty of the forest and approaching the cozy cottage that faced a sandy beach and a quiet placid lake. I always loved to walk on sandy beaches coming from the north and Lake Agatha with its miles of sandy beach encompassing the grandeur of the largest lake on a lake system. It was clear that this place meant a lot to Tom where he had spent many years of his life here.

I walked with Tom to the cottage, a lovely but worn wooden structure all painted white with red trim. It conjured up the feeling of a true cottage encased with many treasured white birch trees that were examined for disease as we came to the front door. We entered the well-lived-in main room that was divided by a fireplace of incredible stone and windows overlooking a beautiful view of the so-serene lake. The furniture was tired and tattered. The water was drawn from the lake with a pump handle—so ornate. Tom's Mom had busied herself in the kitchen preparing a meal. As soon as the meal was done, Tom's father got up to tackle his many chores: the first, to go and get minnows for his passion of fishing. I helped clean-up the kitchen and had the chance to chat with Tom's Mom, who delighted in her children and grandson and other siblings. She was a sweet woman and we had many things in common including dying our hair of which I attempted servicing her that night. A good job but no gloves and I had dyed hands. It seemed almost an enmeshed family—and probably was.

Tom had mentioned the cottage often over the short time I had known him. It was a family gathering place since they were small children. In fact, Tom described many defining moments of his life back to the family cottage on Ball Lake—as did his brothers and sisters. The cottage precedented a certain culture to their family and ultimately all the children had a cottage of their own. It was really a place that enmeshed this family as I would find out later. No real room for others emotionally. No real cottage activities took place: no boat, bikes or even cards. Much chat about each other. The cottage would go on to be a sensitive legacy with much conflict.

In the evening, Tom and I walked the sandy shores hand-in-hand enjoying a beautiful sunset. This was a precious spot for Tom or maybe a trap that compelled you back every weekend to walk and talk about each other and compete.

My very Catholic northern family was close knit but in an open way. I was raised in Moncton, Ontario a northern town famous for the largest set of locks in the world. My father had grown up in the area but my Mom came from the U.S.—moving from various spots and landed in Moncton. My grandfather had been a logger. My siblings (two brothers) attended the same school of the Sacred Heart. I was the middle child of three with a younger brother, Larry, and my older brother, Herbert, named after my paternal grandfather. It was because of the boys and with hockey being an entrenched northern Canada's sport that I enjoyed skating on the rink that my Dad would make every year and from time to time got to be the goalie for a pick-up team.

My brothers and I had a childhood that was happy, safe and secure. There was always kids everywhere to play hockey or softball in the large acre of land next to our home. We walked six blocks to school and came home every day for lunch even in the cold of winter. We had cousins just one block from our house. Every Sunday was a family gathering dinner with my grandmother, aunts and their kids. I never felt lonely just happy and lucky. I always knew I wanted to be a nurse especially as my paternal grandmother grew old and I would assist my Dad to care for her. Life was simple but everyone cared for each other. Family traditions and celebrations were extremely important to me—birthdays, anniversaries, Christmas, Easter and our Sunday get-togethers. My youngest brother was the white-haired knight who ended up with very changing international jobs but affected his life later on with anger management problems.

I never felt that we were privileged but comfortable. My father was a Master Mariner by profession and had been Captain of large freighters and ultimately of the ferries that took you to the U.S.A. My father was also founder of the M.S. View, a boat that took tourists to sightsee the Great Lakes. He was an idol in my eyes and especially when he wore his uniform. My father started from nothing, losing his father in a mine accident at the age of five, leaving school as a very young man and worked at logging with his uncle. He worked his way up to Master Mariner from the bottom.

My mother was before her time succeeding with a Business School certification. My family never wanted for anything but were driven by "make something of yourself" and positive reinforcement for all achievements no matter how big or how small—always proud grandparents. I worked from a very young age babysitting making enough money to purchase those lovely sweaters one dreams about, etc.

Summers were spent working for my father's business while enjoying the perks of Moonlight Excursions on the "M.S. View" with friends on the beautiful St. Helen's River. These boat rides were always accompanied by live music or recorded with space adequate on the main deck for dancing. These excursions were a luxury but we lived otherwise very modestly. Biking was also a great sport in the summer. Sometimes taking us to a bubbling stream where we would fish and picnic—mostly my young brother and I.

I was my father's protege, a gentle man with an extreme work ethic, working as Manager of an International Company and his own business on the "M.S. View" tours. I considered my father a man of great integrity and honesty and early on thought I recognized that in Tom but have been sadly disappointed not only in his standards but in my kid's after my forty years of consistent parenting, adjusting as they grew, university, marriage, grandparenting, and spiritual exposure of the Roman Catholic Church through my beliefs.

The original principles that first drew me to Tom changed dramatically in our elder years. Certainly no family is perfect but these misbehaviours of his family seem excessive to me and were preventable with a little thinking and caring.

# CHAPTER 2

# The Courtship

Soon after my return from the visit with Tom's family, he called me to have a date but I had plans with others to visit the Winter Carnival in Michigan where my younger brother was attending university with a goal to be an engineer. Thereafter, Tom became more attentive, phoning early to line up a date. Thereafter, he drove 90 miles from Unico to my home town.

As we got to know each other better and exchange intimate letters, it became clear that we were growing closer to each other and his goal to go back to University in September to work towards an MBA was disclosed. By March 1960 he had proposed and bought an engagement ring which did not come with a celebration—just a request and an order about his goals—that was a red flag that I missed. We planned the wedding for August—just before he would be leaving his job and going to school. It was a passionate relationship of kissing, fondling but no sex. The ring was smashing and the dress had a sweeping effect with a crinoline under it. It still hangs in the closet. Uncles, aunts, cousins, the whole family came and had a great time eating, dancing and chatting with one another.

I had a great job in nursing as a Supervisor of a 50 bed ward of the General Hospital and loved my position. My father tried to persuade me to let Tom go off to school and when he was finished, get married. I thought I could walk away from this job without regrets but the transformation of living 500 miles from home in a motel-size apartment and a shared washroom and no job was a difficult adjustment for me.

I then pursued a position at both hospitals landing one in Pediatrics which was only for three months as University finished the first semester and we were heading home in our poorly-heated Volkswagen for Christmas. I started there with great references but three months and leaving scarred my reputation somewhat—getting part-time in return.

"Please use only two pieces of toilet paper" was an order I ignored but shocked me. Financially we were poor and Tom was notoriously frugal and controlling. An extreme budget was necessary and I had sold my car and had a savings account and entered the marriage with $2,500 that pooled towards Tom's education. The new medical ward was boring by comparison and did not make use of any exemplary skills. The marriage did not start out as one from heaven as I had a miscarriage on our Christmas trip.

It was a frenzied time but I would look to Tom coming home after a hard day of studying, smart sense of humour and exceedingly handsome with his large blue eyes.

The University life was great fun. Fraternity parties and meeting very interesting new people like Pete with great life goals and who continues to keep in touch and includes his wife Ruth.

Every couple brings individual perspectives and experience to the marriage. Tom and I were the same. I had a tendency to trust the future where Tom was intense about setting goals with no flexibility. It was not as if I did not meet my persona and became a Registered Nurse to help people but it had many options and securities. I looked forward to being a mother and start a family as I got married. It was a challenge I wanted to go meet adding to the fun family I already had. Our relationship was really built on hot and heavy emotions but the 50's shun sex before marriage as did my Catholic conscience. It was great to be married. Those feelings were mutual goals and we enjoyed a good sex life and a touching love which my Mom would say "can't you keep your hands off each other?" This lasted for many years but money was always a conflict. What happened, I do not know! My life goal would be well lived by me having children and a husband happy and well adjusted each seductive in their own way hopefully through their compassions. Also, I had entrenched in my blood to accomplish worthy causes for the needy. Helping people. I inherited that from my Dad who helped the Native Indians from the Reserve giving them jobs.

Possibly, where we went wrong was not to visit our goals from time to time and see if we were on course. Although Tom had benchmarks for himself that I admired, they excluded family as primary and he was profoundly restless and critical of staff in his many jobs that jumped into leaving me with many moves. We moved into new places in nine years; he never finished his MBA as I got pregnant and we had no money so he carried a grudge. Tom always set the bar for financial worth very high born from his father.

Faith had been a constant in my life coming from a Roman Catholic family and educated by the St. Joseph and Grey Nuns of the Immaculate Conception. Blessing before meals, bedtime prayers, crucifixes on the wall. It was as if someone was looking over you from above. Sunday mass was always an unquestioned event for my paternal grandmother who often had the priest at her home as I would drop in from school. The Sacred Heart School and Church are indelible in my mind. First communion, confirmation, Sunday mass and the church that my parents exchanged their marital vows.

Tom clarified his thoughts about my religion as disbelief and although it was a disappointment, Father Gray, the parish priest, said he would marry us because of my strength and raising in the Catholic religion. Tom proclaimed he shared the same values of our religion but not the doctrine, especially the concept of the Trinity but kids could be raised Catholic.

Nevertheless, there was an energized emotion between the two of us and I decided to go ahead with a Catholic-condoned wedding by Father Gray, who knew my family and me not only as a churchgoer but a highly respected Registered Nurse at the Catholic hospital. Religion was a contemptuous issue from time to time in early marriage.

Although Tom rejected some doctrine in the Catholic religion, he agreed to all the Catholic scripture in the marital vows. I know many men doubt themselves but I felt Tom would be faithful and allow children to be raised Catholic. Tom could even quote some of the verses from the Bible that I had been versed and taught through catechism.

I stated to Tom that I believed in marriage as a lifetime commitment and that I was deeply in love with him and the vows would demonstrate that in front of God, family, friends and our loyal attendants, Molly, Mary (my sister-in-law), Alicia, Ted, Robert and Henry. I was always surprised that his brothers were not close enough to Tom to be attendants nor even best man. Love translated to abuse over the last forty marital years—on a gradual basis.

In retrospect, how do you know what the future holds for a couple so in love? Re-reading the courting letters from Tom after a divorce, some 40 years ago, defines some doubt at that time that I never realized. Naivety and love are blind. (See reference.)

In the homily by Father Gray, he spoke of the importance of responsibility and caring for each other. He alluded to the bride as a strong Catholic person that could carry the religion which would help us in good times and bad. You begin the journey together and it is up to two people to keep it on track even as children enter the union.

The whole ceremony put much of the responsibility on the bride who took it seriously and always carried more than her share realizing the large job endowed on her shoulders. This, however, is somewhat normal of the 1960's. Women did it all and men were to be waited on and provide financially for the family, but we did have a great love for each other for many years and that kept it emotionally stable. Money was the man's responsibility.

# CHAPTER 3

## The Marriage

The first days and weeks after the wedding, I looked forward to being blissfully in love forever. A beautiful wedding, and a great honeymoon, and so attracted to one another. Our courtship had been weekends as Tom worked 100 miles away in Unico, a small town. Romantic letters were exchanged in our absence over a period of two years. Now off to University for Tom to do post-graduate work to enhance his education as an engineer.

Tom carried me over the threshold in the traditional way into the apartment he had rented and I virtually was in shock: early Salvation Army furniture, a Murphy bed that folded into the wall allowing sitting room on the couch. As I scouted around for a bathroom, Tom said: "across the hall."

"Sharing a bathroom!" I had lived in a big home with all the amenities. I said: "I can make do any place after all I shared a small room with three nurses for three years." "A motel and eight months is not a long time to function in a place like this," I stated with the love I had for him in my voice.

"Believe me, Hon, I tried but there is no occupancy anywhere especially for couples on the University campus and student budgets."

As a nurse, I had learned to go with the flow. You open your heart to change.

We settled in and decided that a television would help so purchased a very small one that would fit. The oven door could not be opened if one sat on the chairs and that was accompanied by a very small table supposedly to eat our meals. We also discovered that our neighbour was a house of Prostitution.

This dismal grey house also did not have a laundry room—the washing machine and the dryer had blown up and smoked the place out so one must use the laundromat at the corner. A hangout that I found myself visiting often but love will keep everything positive. I also met many interesting people as I awaited for the clothes to dry and Tom to come home from school. I had great confidence in Tom that this was the right thing to do, as I had put all my cash towards his education. The college parties were a hoot and we met many cohorts in similar positions. One cool thing to do for poor students was to go to the Farmers' Market on weekends and pig out on donuts or go for a beer.

There was little time to actually get to know each other but the sexual attraction, sexual life and young love was still great but marriage did not seem enough as I had thought . . . I was bored.

Being 26 years old and an experienced nurse, I set off to get an interview with the St. Joseph's Hospital and landed a job in Pediatrics having pleased them with a great resume.

I was unsure about Tom's reaction as he agreed with his father's philosophy that women belonged in the home and education was a waste as they just get pregnant. We had our first fight but I went to work.

Christmas came and time to go home and apprehension set in as I negotiated with the hospital for days off as Tom had two weeks off. I was not guaranteed a position on my return.

Off we went to Springtown, our first stop, to visit with Tom's family exchanging gifts, laughing and having great fun with Tom's five siblings, his mother Rose, his Dad Edgar, and Jimmy, his nephew. About to leave for my home town, we discovered the little old Volkswagen, our means of transportation, had no defrost or heat, but being in love and jovial, did not take it too seriously even in below zero weather by opening the window and warming our feet by using the bricks heated by Tom's Mom. We were sure happy to reach our destination. Winters up north are cold but fun as rinks hold the freezing, allowing us to get out and skate. The turkey is Christmas to my Mom and we had the biggest and best. Capt. L.B., my Dad, said: "Bless us all," and we overate.

Time to return to school for the final semester at University, so we packed up our wee car that was overloaded with goodies. The trip was uneventful with lots of snow and the poor little car struggled in some places but Tom saw us through and we arrived home safely.

"Four months to go," I said to Tom, "and we have met many new folks with such different professional backgrounds." We will miss them but promised to keep in touch. Tom was a shit disturber at most parties so could not be forgotten too soon. The big drive now was to get a job.

I returned to the hospital for the months ahead and tolerated the jobs on an on-call basis but found it frustrating from time to time as one shift might be Surgical and another Pediatrics leaving me in a continuous orientation mode after eight years of more structure and responsibility in the General Hospital at my previous employ.

Tom graduated from University with his MBA1 with some satisfaction accepting a job in Anitou in northern Ontario. Another move for us. Tom had a restless and somewhat dissatisfied temperament that left us not celebrating accomplishments as I would like to. "He needs a lot of attention," said my Mom—many times.

I had discovered that marriage was not as cozy as I had dreamed and that great love and passion was essential to hold any marriage together. The 60's did not embrace women's rights—another road block.

I can only describe our first year of marriage as a new challenge to me, with many new adjustments to adapt to as we got to know each other. We were both very healthy, educated beings and had to think of building our life together with compromise. Tom started exploring jobs with building a resume that would lead to his goal of status and money. He carried his extreme competitive role with him—his paternal legacy.

We moved to Anitou, a mining town in northern Ontario, that would recognize his skills as an engineer to supervise construction and promised me a job at the small but active northern outpost hospital that would prove to be very challenging with malpractice and questioned quality of medical care.

From the beginning at Anitou, I knew Tom's heart and soul was not engaged as he criticized the Chief Engineer, and his restless dissatisfaction grew. We were hardly settled into this small yellow bungalow with aluminum siding when the phone rang and a voice said "I am Grace, the Directors of Nurses at the hospital and I understand that you are the new Registered Nurse?"

"Yes, I responded.

"Could you report on duty tomorrow as we are desperate for nurses and the salary is bonused by 50% because of the wilderness environment."

I replied, "I will report to the hospital to assume duty nurse as requested."

The first shift on duty was to an immediate question of poor quality care and practices lacking any principles and standards. The case of a bleed resulting from incompetency of cauterization and was not breathing due to blockage of his airway. I picked up the 5-year-old boy and ran to the OR to get suction to unblock the passage which was successful. After my first incident, I chatted with other nurses who suggested other procedures with poor outcomes. Surgical Procedures were happening by a surgeon that was a drug addict, without the proper skill set and assisted by a young very inexperienced physician that lacked any sense of risk management and occupational health and safety. Dr. Grey and Dr. Creation were there visibly for the financial remuneration. I went home after an unconscionable shift and to talk to my beloved husband but he was not on the same page and was at the mine for his career. "Quit," said he, "we can certainly live on my salary." I replied, "with difficulty," and the discussion ceased. To this point in our marriage and courting relationship when things were not right we just fixed them. After considerable conversation, it became clear to me that henceforth I should slip into a hybrid life of support as the wife and be mother to the child that I found myself pregnant with.

Having learned Principles and Practices in a Catholic Hospital, administrated by the Grey Sisters of the Immaculate Conception with a long and thorough dedication to quality assurance and nurses that graduated, were exemplary. This was a traumatic shock to me and my professionalism. I must do something and I must remember my Florence Nightingale pledge as I reasoned to myself and listening to other nurses about the care of patients but their primary goals were to work for a defined time and continue their travel as single gals. Their secondary goal was the patient and had done many interventions for multiple patients. My heart was for the sick as this was not a choice job I found myself in.

A phone call from a Dr. Herrington at the Port Arthur General with good news, Bobby did have Whooping Cough and is now on proper medication and should be home soon. This was great news. Bobby was a happy ending but it would take two years of considerable malpractice incidences, advocacy, and these doctors would be dismissed.

I was very interested in the opportunity to make some money after just being out of University, leaving us cash poor and also to occupy my times in a desperate place without radio, television, a small church, a small school, a curling rink for entertainment and inclement weather twelve months of the year. I felt sometimes all the efforts were for Tom.

From my home town, I ordered and paid for, furniture to make this small white bungalow comfortable. I had never used a needle and thread before but learned quickly to cover the overexposed windows. I think this set a precedent for the financial negotiations in the household. He was in charge.

Although we were both committed to this move to support his career, Tom realized that I had never lived in the bush or even a cottage but this was a definite part of his DNA. The weather was the coldest in the winter in all of Ontario and bugs were so plentiful that no one grew grass in the summer. A car would not start in winter unless the battery was plugged in. We learned to entertain ourselves and shortly the single nurses were hanging out at our house meeting many of the single engineers. Parties, cards, fishing and Bridge were the fun with the great people we met and still connect. The negative side to this experience was Tom who always had to drink himself into oblivion and became sarcastic as a sense of wit. On many occasions, I felt embarrassed. It could ruin the day but it was because of discontent with his work and maybe himself.

One of his claims to fame was expelling a flatus that could empty a room but always award him attention. He also thought he had an entitlement to be rude because he came from an abusive background. He hated his father all his life for abuse but never elaborated on specifics. I was always so proud of my Dad and his caring and giving attitude and always a gentleman, and Tom was always challenging and he ridiculed people. My mother had figured him out and would call him an "insulting pup" but I loved him anyhow. Tom never offered his gratitude only indifference.

I knew in my heart at the age of 26 that I was ready to start my own family and had established a career and sowed my oats but Tom was not—degrees and certifications meant everything to him. He had also established a career but it was not enough.

In Anitou, I became pregnant with our eldest daughter after a serious miscarriage. The doctors working in the hospital were not qualified for the care needed so we drove some 400 miles to my home town in Ontario for care through devastating storms. Anne was born 7 lbs. 1 oz. after struggling for a normal birth ending up in a C Section and thanks to my sister-in-law working as a special nurse to help me to get through. Tom was no place to be found.

In the interim, Tom had found a job in Quebec which he thought would challenge his career objectives. Ten days post-delivery with Anne, I was flying on my way to a small Quebec town with my post-op beautiful daughter and my Mom. What a challenging journey marriage has offered in our three years together. I was happy but anxious with certain set goals for the future. I was a strong woman—thanks to my Mom and Dad and my nursing education.

The first house in Quebec needed to be immediately renovated for a baby soon to crawl. It was located in the Francophone area so soon Tom and myself were using dictionaries to shop and obtain baby's necessities. The French are celebrants and celebrate everything like St. Baptiste Day making it a welcoming place for us Anglos with small children. J.M. Company had hired several new engineers to work. The families became great friends with a commonality of English speaking and all young children.

Six months into living in Quebec, we moved again to a company house of which the company had rooms painted, wallpaper hanging and light fixtures to satisfy our entourage. I even remember "Fred" the man responsible for the company houses saying, "Your husband better stay with all these household improvements costing for the company." As he stated this, I was dreading having the complaints from Tom and knew in my heart that it would not last. I had just learned to Curl and loved the sport while meeting new and lovely people.
In the end, my responsibility in the marriage was working too hard, getting exhausted, keeping two places thus a lack of any connection with Tom.

Just about two years later and still very much in love, we were off to a new town in southern Ontario realizing the need for her husband to carve out another niche. A company called P.D.M., dealing with synthetics, was this new endeavour and I supported it realizing his frustration to fill his need.

We moved into a rented side split house and a neighbourhood where resided many small children for Anne to play with. She also enjoyed two hours a week of Child Resource Centre with other kids. Early on I had learned to sew on a second-hand machine to clothe Anne and myself. Tom was frugal and so money was tight. The stock market was mentioned in passing from time to time as a dream for Tom. I should have questioned.

Mother became pregnant with a sister for Anne while Tom hashed away at trying to meet his dream at his new position.

The pregnancy brought morning sickness and pica—not a good thing but tolerable. Having one child and one on the way made sense to settle down and having a home. Hudson Street, it was a beautiful home and we moved as I went to the hospital to have a testy C Section with an evisceration of my incision to deliver our second daughter, Carey, but it ended up well even though Mom hardly made it. A darling baby girl with such a beautiful temperament. As she grew, people would comment on this happy baby and toddler.

Tom travelled to Europe in those days for the company and with two kids found it lonely. Social life was enhanced by house parties and Bridge.

When Carey was two and Anne close to five, there were rumblings of the company downsizing which scared us. A shortage of one salary and my skill set degenerating in a one-company town.

Talk was necessary for a future. I had heard there was a Medical Centre opening close and cogitated a possible job or move before the house market got glutted from company shifts.

Tom had talked about the stock market briefly at one point so I pushed the button as I was frightened of unemployment. He scanned the newspapers and sought out job opportunities in Toronto as a Stock Analyst. Job interviews went well but we had to sell the house in southern Ontario. We painted it through and in one week sold it and travelled to Toronto after accepting a job at a small security business to find a house with a mortgage higher by some 15% growing Tom an ulcer but purchased a home. The present family home on Black Drive in Toronto allowing him great public transportation.

As we moved into this home, I promised myself for the sake of family, stability and the cyclical business Tom was in that I would never move again and I would pursue my career as a Registered Nurse as soon as the children would become old enough to be more independent.

The job restlessness carried on in Toronto with Tom challenging many Brokerage Houses and banks but soon exhausted these opportunities and he became a consultant Incorporating as TMC.

When Carey was ten and Anne twelve, I decided to pursue my career returning to Toronto General Hospital associated with a College to refresh and upgrade my Registered Nurse promising myself some stability for my kids and sanity for myself.

Tom threw himself into consulting, travelling, writing reports and had great credentials with his degreed certifications that he acquired studying evenings which gave him a challenge.

The Stock Market has a certain culture of its own and Tom adapted the "make money" philosophy, lots of drinking and the excitement of the stock market which was his niche but separated and disconnected our relationship somewhat The social outings became business development and questioned my values of all work and no play. Couple Curling became obsolete because of the career commitments as did Bridge.

As the kids grew and an empty nest developed, I became more involved in community services (History Addendum) with a husband engrossed in his niche and making money and building a cottage that would outdo all his family of origin.

In many ways, it was hypocritical as Tom never recognized my participation financially or even my successes as a Registered Nurse paying for the necessities: food, clothing and furniture, while he played the market and less writing reports the object of his consulting practice and incorporation.

Our relationship and love was lost in the shuffle of his dream—money, and I did not realize this was happening. In final analysis, it was the traditions and expectations that we had inherited from our families that highlighted our differences. There comes a time when all things end but I believed we could grow old together even with such great differences—another fallacy. Now we had money, fair health and travel for fun after all these years—it would not happen.

# CHAPTER 4

## The Children/Grandchildren

By the time we had our last move, I was enchanted with newfound joys of motherhood and enjoying every minute of crafts, baking cookies, making Halloween outfits and enjoying other kids on the street. Also, I was developing new relationships with mothers' kids the same age as Anne and Carey in our new home. The next door neighbours had boys the same age as our kids and we had transported a full-blown Play House from our last home that all the kids adapted as their nucleus for play.

The house was great for raising kids: a dead end with little traffic and a big yard that would eventually have climbing bars, swing set and a large pool. We air-conditioned the house for comfort and did a gradual job on painting indoors, wall-to-wall rugs making it a good and comfortable place to build a family. A whole lot of good things and very little bad. It was stability to me—I would stay here and continue to this day.

Pinewood offered us as a family, a rich life with community and families. It was located in a community of its own within the largest city of Canada. A place unto itself. Kids could bike on their own, go shopping with friends. Bridge, Curling and entertaining were great outlets for me while attempting to involve Tom but his restlessness was awakened again and he needed more stimulation studying for his CFA.

I love consistency in my life and I felt this house location would give this to me with continuous loving and living and building a family and associating with a community. "It takes a community to build a family." A constant in one's life, and we had it. I was always happier when our home was full of kids and friends. I even taught ceramics in my home.

Pinewood Day with its parades allowing kids to decorate their tricycles and bicycles with entertainment all day and dance and food at night. I had so much pride and respect for my kids to decorate their bikes and ride to such perfection.

We had really moved in this bright community to accommodate transportation for Tom. Twenty-five minutes to work with multiple choices to enhance his career at the Financial Stock Brokerage Centre. Any challenge he desired but constant dissatisfaction. I should have listened to him more.

Prince Simcoe was the Primary School from Kindergarten to Grade 8 of which both kids enjoyed and excelled working together as a parent and teacher along with the principal. A team approach and a community. At one time, I took a child into our home that her parents had left her to enhance the father's job and relied on older kids as her guardians. It did not work and I took her into my home. I always tried to teach my kids to give back while giving back and I loved my children to stay home and do without to love and raise them.

Extra-curricular activities were included in both kids' lives and gave them exposure and test their skill set: piano, organ, ballet dancing, guitar, figure skating and baton. We could afford these extra luxuries for both kids because Mom sewed all their clothes. A skill set she acquired early on when Anne was a babe without a wardrobe. In fact, it became a great education component escalating to sewing designer clothes for myself, and quilting on a very limited budget to meet Tom's fiscal philosophy.

Kids are new, refreshing and so present in the world and that is why I miss my grandchildren. We as elders have been there. The kids always looked great—sometimes alike that became a delicate subject later on while striving for individuality. The only two label dresses they owned were through the generosity of their maternal Grandma Bertha. She loved them and had fun with both kids. She even travelled with us from time to time and had a great time.

I believe the most important thing you can do is instill confidence in your kids so they can fare in life as I did. That was integrated in my parenting.

Being a father was not a primary function for Tom but I tried to empathize and support his need to settle his spirit. As his wife, I sensed some frustration and shared it in a way, absorbing what I could from him but unable to treat whatever it was that enhanced his anxiety. In a conversation I had with his Dad one time, he alluded to getting help for his anxiety attacks at a mental institution. Maybe Tom needed the therapy as well. He said he was full of bottled-up rage. I listened but did not ask why!

On many occasions, Tom and I talked in depth about his discontent with his bosses' social networking always blaming them. I engaged in attending annual conventions, engaging with folks that would help Tom meet his career objectives and give him more exposure. I also entertained business folks attempting to give him support but never seemed to energize and focus him to happiness. I was naive—he needed to do it himself or get help, but my friends still say the parties were great and we did have fun and gave an excellent opportunity for connection.

Enjoying your work is critical for happiness. Meanwhile, parenting and raising two very intelligent daughters continued with Anne excelling from Kindergarten to Grade 1 in her first year. It was not without Mom tutoring her in good work habits that she succeeded. Carey became my little buddy in her preschool times—assisting me with grocery shopping, etc. while actively playing with her best male friend—GI Joe became her favourite. Anne was a lover of Barbie. Very young, both kids achieved skating and swimming. A joy to watch as I did not swim coming from the northern country but did skate very well and thrilled kids on the ice while playing "Crack the Whip." Most Moms give their all for a good life and safety of their children. Another factor that bound the family and shaped character was the dog. It was not a consensus for Tom but I did it and he lived 14 glorious years of our kids' life.

However, the disruption of the presence of children enhances the marriage but also adds to a new challenge, and a whole new family values document which I found exciting—that includes religion with baptism, communion, confirmation and gaining a spiritual side of our children. It also was important to engage my kids with grandparents, aunts, cousins of which I did often to keep nurturing extended family—travelling numerous times.

Holidays with kids from the start gave great diversity and fun. The first camping trip in a tent found Anne sleeping in a puddle of water. It had rained all night and evidently we did not recognize the need to be on higher ground as a prevention. Upgrading to a tent trailer gave as many exciting vacations in Nova Scotia, New Brunswick, Florida and many others. One that was a defining moment in my life was Disneyland which I longed to return to just have a peek at the amazement in the eyes of my grandchildren, but a simple process became the most overreacted incident I ever witnessed as if I would ruin the vacation of Anne's in-laws. A behaviour and decision I still do not logically understand.

One winter sport we enjoyed as a family was cross-country skiing. Children grow so fast and before long it was time for kids to change schools. Anne to Louise High School and Carey to middle school, Northern Miner. Both kids would graduate with provincial scholarships ultimately and boyfriends came and went. Anne being a bit of a klutz led Mom to engage her in a modelling school which proved timely for mother waiting around places like the Royal York, etc. Carey would excel in playing in the band at Northern Miner and cross-country running. The thrill to Mom was music she loved but could not even hum a note. The most was "Jesus Christ, Superstar" and I would cry—my daughter playing the horn.

When Carey turned ten, she was the leader of the crossing guard school team I decided to refresh my nursing to get a job. Simultaneously, the idea of camping became obsolete with Tom and kids too big so cottage hunting was the next phase and we purchased a make-over on Blue Lake. A project for Tom, a joy for kids to boat, water ski and have teenage life full of lake activities and new fun and friends with mutual interests. Carey became a great boater, Anne an excellent water skier, Mom passed her exams while Tom got to use his hammer and tools leaving us with a comfy summer dwelling. The interior became my responsibility using my sewing skills and Salvation Army furniture—a tremendous, pleasant revitalization. No indoor plumbing but that would come later in the years. The dwelling was in the lovely spot that had a small inland lake on which I loved to paddleboat. The neighbours were great having kids of similar age. This make-over cottage was done with limited dollars.

The ideal place and there was something even with mammoth bugs that made it a happy place for all. Projects seemed to give some peace to Tom for a while. He had also achieved three projects at the home in Toronto. We all want the best things in life to stand still but soon it came time for Anne to go to University in the Bachelor of Finance which seemed to match her academic high quotient in math and Carey was well liked in high school. Anne carried on with her boyfriend with questionable ambition from Grade eleven but we continued to welcome him in our home with his friends eating us out of house and home. Lasagnes just disappeared.

Parenting is a full time job and so is being a wife but kids stay. Men can come and go but children are forever—especially for Moms that had to carry them for nine months. It is wonderful bonding time. Carey developing into a young good looking woman was ready to go off to University to achieve a Bachelor in Science, knowing she would eventually be in the Human Services, medicine, education but kept her options open. During her teen years, it was tough for the family with her profound rebellion against Tom. She called him Thompson to be negative and he did nothing about it. I was the scapegoat and in-between for that escapade and I tried but was re-entering the work force full time with not the height of self-esteem. I had done some menial jobs doing physicals for insurance companies in people's homes but not full-time five days, even overtime to take on the task of actually building a Community Service Organization and attending classes awakening at 5:00 a.m. to upgrade my skills.

My kids were lucky to have the opportunity to give back to society as the Community Services I headed up was volunteer-driven. It also served such high need folks, families, children and both kids experienced volunteerism. My youngest, who became a teacher, led a timework program in housing helping kids in need and they loved her back. My eldest always helped with Operation Christmas—the program that gave and delivered hampers to oppressed families that made their Christmas a delight. I really thought I taught my children to give and not to take as has been demonstrated in the companies' dynamics. Anne even blamed me later on for her negative relationship with her father—unbelievable.

It hurts me every day when I think of the kids supporting the Corporation falsification and how Tom lied about me knowing and understanding all the Corporation changes and laws without legal counsel of my own as his wife. I am so glad at least I had him before the courts regarding anger—a lifetime affliction. Worse things could have happened.

Off to University Carey went, not even to return for summer jobs. Tom and her had a bitterness between them. Anne was about to graduate and decided to be Europe-bound on a cycle tour for six weeks and then she returned to Toronto. I heard from her from time to time. In the meantime, her obtrusive boyfriend left some reminders that he was still alive and well. He sank one boat at the cottage and punctured another. While another University boyfriend was calling me to get permission to fly to Europe to visit her. She was 21—"she made her own decisions" was my response.

Carey came home to state she had met a man and wished to live with him and Tom recoiled and said "no money" and she carried through her plan. Bill moved in. They finished University and moved back to Toronto and got married and within a few years a divorce. I never could reconnect with Carey. I tried with suggesting we take a psyche course together at U of T that would benefit both our careers. It really did not work but gained a wealth of knowledge.

Anne got married the first year after graduation and immediately had a family of three children. By now, we had a new cottage. I tried to help her by weekend respite—kids at the cottage, meeting, eating, other needs and attempting to engage them in the water sports they had so enjoyed. A big boat and a Sea-Doo. I purchased several bikes.

The new abode seemed to satisfy Tom as the old cottage was never enough. It seemed to be his dream picking out every rock. I went along as it was nice to see Tom happy but very tense about every phase in the building process.

I took over the task and payment of decorating the interior. New bunk beds for grandchildren, etc. Tom and I did have fun building the new cottage. It became a family gathering place, a place to have friends and a place for special celebrations. Christmas, birthdays, Easter for a long time were spent at Montebello with a family connected to Tom's work and Spring Breaks in South Carolina. The divorce "craziest ever" ended all that for me.

Anne went on to achieve her MBA, stayed at the cable company becoming a Director. Carey, the degree in education, which ultimately lead to a principalship. In the midst, Carey married again and had two beautiful daughters. She married into a lovely family. Both girls purchased lovely homes which they decorated and made comfortable in which to raise their children but not without financial help.

The grandchildren are interesting. As they grow into responsible adults and being a grandmother is a delight when you see them. Children and grandchildren are a motivator in our lives especially as we grow older and the aging process enters. They give hope and interest into the great challenges of the future for creative jobs, etc.

My children meant so much to me that I even took precaution and did not fly as my husband was always in travel and I did not want to leave two children without at least one parent. In retrospect, there are many times when I feel that I overworked and looking after two houses and full time job and getting older gave me that feeling. No time for personal growth, reflection or to recharge batteries, or marriage growth. Retirement finally came time and then assault and divorce. Never even in my golden years did I realize how uninformed I was especially about Tom's primary love of money, a workaholic with his sense of conspiracy as I went along signing papers without documentation. In fact, one time a slap in my face. I was set up by my husband and kids.

Stupid Smuck. I wonder what went wrong after my 70th birthday. It sure was a self-esteem upper—the birthday logs.

## CHILDREN LEARN WHAT THEY LIVE

If a child lives with criticism, he learns to condemn.
If a child lives with hostility, he learns to fight.
If a child lives with ridicule, he learns to be shy.
If a child lives with shame, he learns to feel guilty.
If a child lives with tolerance, he learns to be patient.
If a child lives with encouragement, he learns confidence.
If a child lives with praise, he learns to appreciate.
If a child lives with fairness, he learns justice.
If a child lives with security, he learns to have faith.
If a child lives with approval, he learns to like himself.
If a child lives with acceptance and friendship, he learns to find love in the world.

## *Happy Birthday, Reasons Why We Love Our Mom*

1. She gave birth to us.
2. She had those really groovy red/white/blue flip up sun glasses.
3. She wore cool plaid "safari suits" during the 70's and has always kept up on fashion.
4. She made us matching bikinis to wear.
5. She got us a dog, and then another one when he turned out to be mean when poked incessantly by Anne.
6. Took care of the "damn dogs" even when they are "pains in the a." and defended our right to dress Noel in baby clothes and walk him down the street in a doll carriage.
7. She taught us how to swim.
8. She took us on all kinds of family vacations that Anne remembers fondly. Carey still has her Mickey Mouse ears.
9. She came to Carey's track meets.
10. She drove Carey and her friends to the various cross-country track meets all over Toronto.
11. She enrolled us in piano, gymnastics, and ballet just to see what our shining talents were.
12. She came on school trips and always volunteered to take the challenging boys.
13. She took us, our friends, our cousins to the Ex every year, as well as Ontario Place, Marineland, African Lion Safari, the zoo, the zoo in the Soo, etc., etc., etc., etc.
14. She made us groovy clothes like knee length vests to go with our mini skirts and white go-go boots.
15. She helped Anne pass Grade 1 doing homework every night and learn good work habits . . . so that by Grade 2, she was accelerated!!
16. She shopped tirelessly with us for the perfect fitting pair of jeans.
17. She taught us how to do ceramics.as well as most of Carey's friends.
18. She bought us a cool dune buggy that scared her to death whenever we drove it.
19. She brought the grandkids the greatest toys including the train and the kiddie jeep.
20. She sang loudly and proudly at church every Sunday that she did not have a stomach ache.

21. She dressed for school pick-ups—always a bandanna over her curlers to match her plaid suits.
22. She insisted we get our teeth fixed by Dr. Vanach! Now we get compliments on our fabulous teeth.
23. She watched Anne in parades with her baton no matter how cold and bitter the weather was.
24. She wasn't afraid to "do our hair up"—Anne's fabulous perm and Carey's helicopters.
25. She is a good sister to her brothers and their families.
26. She decorates the home and cottage spectacularly for all holidays and celebrations!
27. She can always be counted on for solid medical advice or direction.
28. She left tags on our Christmas presents when we became finicky teens so we always got to dress cool.
29. She always believed in us. defended Anne against her Grade 10 wacko Geography teacher—defended Carey against the Vice-Principal who wrongly accused her of "graffiti" on the lockers.
30. She baked dessert every night.
31. She always carries Tylenol, Caladryl, band-aids, etc.... now so do her daughters.
32. She kept frozen goodies in the house at all times (cookies, Kit Kat bars, O'Henry bars, hamburgers and spaghetti.
33. She let Carey have lunch on her own at home when the neighbour's hospitality wore thin for Carey.
34. She let Carey wear groovy jeans and clogs when all the other kids weren't allowed to.
35. She enrolled Anne in summer school to "keep her out of trouble" and let her swim at a criminal's house every day after summer school.
36. She made sure we were safe and test drove our boyfriends' driving abilities before we could get in the car.
37. She taught us how to drive the boat cautiously and safely ... we always abided ... in the bay!
38. She made sure we got our beauty sleep—if it was late and we were outside with a boy she flicked the lights until we came in to get our beauty sleep.

39. She used tough love when needed—threatened to kick Anne out of the home unless she started to behave and forbade her to hang out with Charlene Simpson—a bad influence.
40. She has a hardy laugh!
41. She made sure Carey got taken to a Toronto hospital when she fell off the horse . . . Thank goodness!!
42. She let us have friends over all the time even those with "bottomless pits" for stomachs, so she could know all our friends and know where we were and who we were with.
43. She let Kristie Brown live with us when her parents went to the U.S.
44. She sent Carey to Europe to have a special trip with her big sister.
45. She always had gifts for us when she went away on business trips with Dad and we stayed with Aunt Anne or Grandma B.
46. She was a kind and supportive daughter to Grandma B through all her stages of aging!
47. She sent care packages with cookies, money, etc., etc., to us at University.
48. She took Carey grocery shopping when kindergarten was just too intimidating!!
49. She taught us how to wallpaper/paint a room whenever Dad went hunting.
50. She gave us cars to use while at University.
51. She likes sappy movies.
52. She is an expert boo-boo fixer!!!
53. She has always offered financial support and been generous with gifts for all occasions!
54. She was supportive through all the births of our children.
55. She taught us that a little gargle or a little soak with salt water cures many things!
56. She still makes the best pies ever!!!
57. She taught (at least Carey) how to bake pies, cakes, cookies . . . . etc. She taught Anne how to sew.
58. She was the original neighbourhood "road" watch with her red sweater at the Lake Bridge of the first cottage—Accident Prevention.
59. She made awesome spaghetti and meatballs . . . even Noel the dog couldn't get enough.

60. She has always proudly supported us in our education and career pursuits!
61. She made all our birthday celebrations fun and memorable with games, theme cakes, great activities . . . even for crazy Trevor hiding in the crawl space wearing his Superman cape!
62. She allowed us independence as teenagers and allowed us to learn from our mistakes.
63. She helped us get jobs in MTHA that helped form our character and set foundation for life-long charitable outlooks for all people.
64. She continues to ride her bike!!
65. She learned how to use the computer, including internet, etc., etc.
66. She keeps her hair bright auburn!
67. She rocks as a Grandma and keeps our kids dressed funkily.
68. She loves us for who we are.
69. She continues to challenge her skills, interests and knowledge base.
70. She is feisty!
71. She taught us to stand up and be strong.

Happy Birthday Mom!!!

# CHAPTER 5

## Good Times

Inconsistency in life makes one search out the good times to be positive and have happy days. When I look back on all those wonderful days of Christmas, I remember the gentleness and love that enhanced the environment. Trimming the tree with ornaments that were saved over the years bringing memories of the past. The memories grew from spending Christmas with my folks to always having a spare room for Mom, or better known as Grandma B., to come and celebrate with us.

Who would have thought a family would self-destruct on the impulse of greed for money and suppressed anger that would give a dedicated wife and mother long and difficult grief.

The forty years of great joy were years that I lived fully that I believed life as a continuous celebration of chocolate chip cookies, to attending a formal event, to decorating the whole cottage with branches and bows as Christmas came or coloured eggs galore to celebrate Easter. Great fun. Some difficult times when Grandma B. died but we had her memories.

Regressing back to when Anne took her first step and hit her head on the coffee table or the time that gave me great guilt as she slipped out of my hands as I had greased her too much and down she went. I cannot remember in all the years that I was bored.

The times when Anne would purposely fall down in the snow while cross-country skiing as it was not her favourite sport but we always got her up. The many Halloweens that we created by Mom sewing costumes that would allow the kids to play a different character. Carey's first costume was Little Red Riding Hood sewed very quickly from some old red curtains. It did the trick, she got a great lot of candy. I found pleasure in the small things or whatever I was doing.

My mother, Grandma B., left some wonderful memories. The visit to Mackinaw Island where she decided to rent a three-wheel bicycle and had never rode before. Down she went over an incline and into the lake laughing all the way. Oops—someone forgot to tell her about brakes but steering came natural. On her trip to Sherbrooke, Quebec, she managed to take the wrong bus and landed in Montreal—great shopping anyhow!

For the most part, all our family were well and in high spirits achieving our passions until the secret was disclosed. Money was always an obsession with Tom so I worked and could pay for trips to places like Montebello for Easter celebrations and also on amazing budgets. Paying for groceries, household maintenance like a new fridge so money was not a large problem.
Very early in our marriage, there seemed to be a calming effect in confiding in each other from time to time. After researching and reading the book *If The Man You Love Was Abused* many of his unpredictable attitudes and behaviours were identified after the fact.

Birthdays, anniversaries, special times were occasions to celebrate or just a party for fun. We gathered in homes and took turns. We made our own fun and included neighbours, kids, close friends, relatives and assured that no one was left out. Socialization was seen as important for a healthy life and grandparents were inclusive. My extended family gave great joy to us. My mother's sister Edna could do the "Big Apple" dance and keep us in hysterics. Uncle Bill was a bit bland but loved to go hunting and fishing with my Dad, brothers and his boys. Family around gave us a great feeling of security, accountability and motivated us to do our very best. Family get-togethers were my legacy and initiative from a young age of 10 when I learned to cook.

All these traditions carried on well after marriage and Tom seemed to enjoy them and honoured my way of life, and when the children came they added to the joy on a daily basis. Crafts, making and decorating cakes and cookies, birthday parties with special themes inviting everyone from the street. The family house was always full of kids and fun—even when they returned from University. John, a particular friend of Anne, frequented our home, a kid from a family of seven and savoured my food so much would put his order in often—cakes, cookies.

Skating was a favourite for me playing "Crack the Whip," twirling a line of kids around until they were knocked off. Carey had a friend that moved in to our home at one point. All these inspired events called for positive emotions including love, passion, appreciation, hope, resilience and gratitude. These caused happiness, a good attitude which transferred to the world. As a nurse, I realized the benefits of positivity even when sometimes our trailer trips did not satisfy all—I liked trailering.

After the kids had left for University and ultimately we had exciting and challenging jobs and Tom had job options as he desired, he made a good win on the stock market to allow him to build the cottage of his dreams. It was great fun but crazy as well trying to keep up with contractors, etc. Tom worried because of his extremely frugal habits. We seemed closer than ever when we built this new cottage—like old times. One night we spent in an old motel sleeping on a bed for one but laughed as we tried to turn over and it was so cold we wore our heavy jackets to bed. We also bought a Jeep to cross-country. One day, I was driving and hit an ice patch and started to be out of control. I came within an inch of a head-on to a tree but my first concern was Tom as I held my arm over to his side to save him. I still cared about him no matter what.

We thought this new endeavour would be a place to extend family as it grew. The space was great and had room for three families. A large all-purpose room that was 2000 square feet allowing for a large harvest table seating 12 folks and a bright kitchen designed especially with windows to allow the moon and sun to shine in. I always loved that old cottage and the great noises of kids having fun but a cottage to Tom was like a DNA—and bigger was better.

I had adapted to the new place making friends and joining a Bridge club but Tom had taken refuge in this dwelling semi-retiring four to five days a week but as years passed, he came on his own for the most part and we were sleeping separately at his request because of his extreme snoring and restlessness. When I would work in the city, he would return home late for dinner. It became a more distant relationship for me except for work and friends who filled my time well and when the kids would come and eventually the grandchildren, I felt the feeling of family extension and the large meals enjoyed around the long table which Dan, one of our neighbours, made and referred to it as the "Bowling Alley." All family get-togethers were at the cottage. The family house was foreign to the grandchildren.

When Grandma B. passed on she left money which allowed me to purchase a big boat and Sea-Doo to encourage water fun and a few bikes. I loved biking with the grandkids as they grew older one by one. Great conversations.

A great place for family weekend fun and to entertain friends. Tom's relatives were also welcomed with the best of meals, sleeping accommodation and courtesy and many, many weekends the cottage was full of the noises and cheers of my grandchildren right from the start when the eldest grandson was in my arms. Fireworks were recognized by the whole street as fun for special occasions.

# CHAPTER 6

## The Secret Shame

I always believed that trust and loyalty was at the root of a good marriage and those values came in my case from my parents. I had witnessed that with my parents and in a way with my paternal grandmother as she would tell me the wonderful stories and show pictures of her only love in life, Grandpa Herbert. He had been killed in an accident in his early thirties. It was not blind trust but the kind that comes from supporting each other and which builds a deep relationship. I still am in awe about my husband's actions. A good marriage gives unconditional love, a deep knowledge of each other, and assisting both to succeed in life and I thought I did that expecting to have a lifelong partner to grow old with. Looking back now I see conduct that was bonding started to separate with financial restrains which were by Tom and the kids. In fact it turned out it was the Estate Freeze taking me out of equalization of funds. A plan done purposely some time before. The kids would win and Mom would lose.

The best prediction of future behaviour is past behaviours and although I never understood his verbal abusive remarks. It was probably because I did not know his past. The big secret of abuse. I did not condone autocratic or corporal parenting with our kids and I did achieve that behind-the-door discussions. My mind always remembers the good times but my body still shakes when I see violence and hear verbal abuse and I witnessed violence personally which threw me into traumatic shock and I felt the same way about Tom's sister's disclosure.

Keeping secrets was never one of my better virtues—a total open person. In fact the words of my mother still ring in my ears: "Can't you keep anything to yourself. It is sometimes smart to have knowledge others do not know." I also had a great sense of trust and honesty almost to stupidity, she would remind me. So was it any wonder that I did not suspect that my husband was a survivor of childhood abuse. His young brother Peter was sympathetic when he visited once or twice and we visited him in prison. It was not discussed. There were signs with unwarranted anger through the years that stood in the way of effective communication, constant discontent with employment, lacking self-esteem and a deep hate for his father. I conducted myself as usual: non-judgmental, accepting of his behaviour, a good listener and allowing most of his needs to supersede mine. We did disagree to agree from time to time was my pact. Positive reinforcement. I shall never forget the day of the childhood abuse disclosure as it came from his sisters. We were all sitting around the table at the cottage. His sisters, Marie and Ala with their husbands, and Tom and myself enjoying a drink of wine and general chatter when Marie blurted out that "the world has changed and the topic of family incidences were now acceptable to discuss and she did not want to suffer her hurt anymore." Tom said, "What are you talking about, Marie?"

"I am talking about our Dad and how he sexually used me!" said Marie.

Annette blurted out: "I did not know it happened to you as well."

A dead silence fell over the cottage. I felt that she needed warmth, a hug but felt Tom should take some of these initiative as it was his family.

Marie went on to explain that she was in treatment with medications after suffering from many unknown anger rages, anxiety attacks and depression and was referred to a psychiatrist as her actions had a serious impact on her family. Annette also shared her treatment and similar experiences. The verbal and physical abuse was also discussed by both girls with my husband who was in complete denial. Thirty-five years of marriage and suddenly some insight into his unexplainable intermittent behaviour. The eldest had attempted suicide by cutting many times and was in a psychiatric facility twice. Tom remained in denial and avoidance which caused some stress and conflict to me.

The time we went to visit his father in a nursing home to attempt to reconcile and the hostile position he took was unbearable. I had thought that Tom should get the weight off his shoulders and a visit would lead to an open discussion with some real exchange. Tom took his chair and turned it around in the most defensive position. No connection only his father defending the good things he did—loaning money to his daughters and son David, etc. There were no emotional outbursts or actual acts of abuse except for the tension in the air that could be cut with a knife. Tom hated his father until he died. His Dad even called the night before he died and no emotion on Tom's part. Heavy anger and hate until the end. Tom never did disclose, in fact, what his anger was all about. What was his abuse—verbal, physical, part of the secret unknown to the day?

The time his Dad visited Tom's work, he found his father so-called overbearing personality and came home in a hostile mood because of his Dad's behaviour. "Asking too many questions," he said, "embarrassing him."

Tom disliked any kind of authority because as a kid he was ruled in his childhood home. The police he called pigs for no reason and even standing in a theatre to the "Queen" he refused to stand and honour. This anger and psychological denial of abuse and avoidance to talk continued. His younger brother David declared that "He knew what was going on" and challenged Tom because of adjacency of bedrooms in a small home of six kids using some choice words. "Jesus Christ, Tom."

The disclosure regarding childhood abuse was a silent pivotal point in the lives of Tom and me and the marriage. For me to know was too much for Tom to accept and our lives changed. He declared the marriage was over and we took separate rooms and that was in 2002. I was so busy keeping two houses and a full time responsible job, I could not keep up the support he needed as I had always done. We still ate together, went places and at our age sleeping in a bed of my own gave my bones the comfort they needed. Tom was also aging with hypertension, the first sign of the body degenerating following in the years with blackouts, many anxieties and by November 2005 had developed unexplainable anger rages inclusive of physical and severe verbal abuse. My suspect was supression as a Registered Nurse that had Mental Health Education and Trauma. When I retired, I attempted to do some interventions on our relationship realizing marriage goes through thresholds and there could salvage and accept the natural changes that happen in marriage and relationships. A trip to Florida, creating new friends and cards but it didn't seem to matter there was no happiness or possible reconciliation. My daughter Carey also was phoning daily on the Florida trip and me never guessing that was part of the conspiracy. The only persons to win in the divorce were my daughters, husband and grandchildren. Again a fortune I did not know about.

It has been said that growing distance does automatically spell disaster but can also be a part of a cycle that returns to redefine the relationship in a new form and recapture even surpass the intimacy they once had as shown in the letters early on. I tried but it was insurpassable. I think the greatest stumbling block was the in-depth psychological hate that Tom held for his Dad and the influence of his two children that saw the Estate Freeze as a huge monumental gain for them and their families and their belief in divorce as the quick answer to marital problems. The eldest daughter had lead the divorce process and the youngest daughter went with it because my eldest daughter had financial skills and my youngest even to net gross salary. My kids were drowning us with negativity for their gains.

I think hate was an infliction and now Tom had misdirected it to me. Father was dead not here to hate. The truth is that anyone that treated his Dad at death as Tom did was questionable as how compassionate he would be to human beings. Edgar's abuse, hitting and beatings, verbal abuse and incest were not Tom's or his siblings' fault. I did what I could do to alleviate abuse responsibility and listen. Talk about it—no success. I knew Tom's father set up competition and judgement with siblings: bigger car, cottages, etc., etc. Tom destroyed his own life as well. He never enjoyed life with me. Tom making Anne be responsible for him because she said "I took away from her having a relationship with him." Tom's influence and "people make their own relationships," said I.

The little secret went on to magnify as others came through with incidents. Annette, his sister, assisted by his mother, followed a detective to prove his father's sexual encounters with other women in Springtown. Tom's Aunt Hattie, sister to Alice, his Mom, talked at length about his father coming on to a sister-in-law and both sisters detailed incest with Tom's father.

In fact, at our wedding, it was said that he came on to my Aunt Louise's neighbour friend and I ignored it. Tom's Dad hid his abuse and compensated his behaviour by being a Director of the Board for Children's Aid Society in

Springtown. In fact, I had forgotten that Tom said many times that in his teens he felt like shooting his father.

Allan (the youngest kid) pulled a knife on a teacher in Grade School. Abuse is terrible but leaves the perpetrator to destroy many people's lives and scars don't go away and causes generation after generation abuse with hate and feelings that do not belong to the victim.

Psychologists say that the worst thing that can happen to a female child is incest and to a woman assault by her husband. Incest was disclosed by Tom's female siblings but I am still mystified how Tom could be so intelligent, conscious of his name and a well-established career in a large city in the finance community and act in such stupid, selfish and destructive way to his family and himself by assaulting his wife to alleviate his frustrations and denial. An assault that must be reported in my opinion as the victim or more serious complications were bound to happen. A man with guns and irrational behaviour. It was a psychological puzzle to me the recipient of the physical choking because I thought I knew him, trusted him but did shockingly find out that I did not understand this man after 40 years of marriage or he had physiological age changes as a result of cardiovascular disease. An unprecipitated, and without cause, misdirected explosion that was suppressed for years accompanied with untreated and undiagnosed disease which I tried to implement with his doctor to differentiate and move towards resolution. I used as much intervention as I knew but it did not work. I even tried to put some fun and romance back into the relationship. It did not work. My kids did not want it or support it because it would not be a gain for them and their families especially my husband who eluded to money or possessions ad nauseum

Assault by my husband was a very debilitating experience that left me initially in a post-traumatic state of shock ceasing to function. Frozen. It is a long process that leaves you with scars that never go away. Because it is your partner the shock is ultra with no support and if he compensates this experience not truthfully chances are other people do not believe you inclusive of your siblings that you gave a large part of your life raising—thus self-doubt. A lack of self-esteem.

I was really ignorant of childhood abusive events of Tom that can leave psychological scars and how it can transfer to the next generation. It took research, reading and therapy to gain knowledge after insight from his sisters' disclosures. I could even be an enabler to Tom's behaviour over the years because I have learned you can't fix it—the abuse has to take responsibility and I felt sorry for him. His ups and downs made me nervous and his extreme hatred for his Dad over the years was without explanation. I realized that his father feared the youngest son and kept a gun for protection but had sought help from a psychologist at Lakeshore Psychiatric Hospital. Over the years, I had suggested to Tom that he get counselling. These were intermittent times between good times and bad. Other than that I felt powerless for his anger and parasitic remarks.

My kids witnessed this behaviour but they did not know or realize the overwhelming parental abuse he suffered from his father nor did I. It was never disclosed by their father only their father's siblings and never in detail by Tom, himself. I have not only been a latent victim but as I look back experienced a lot of hurt and heartbreak when I was put down and deterred it. I was an enabler exacerbating a problem that needed therapy in retrospect

At one point in my Community Services work I ran for government. I thought win, lose or draw, I would raise the awareness in a high-need community but he could only label me as a "loser." I would still like to hear an honest description of Tom's abusive background. I did enable his anger, excusing his verbiage and rages but gradually in the years became tired. The trip to Florida, Tom was still complaining to his Dr., Uncle Thompson, about not being "left in the will from his Dad." Complaining but no realization that he never came to a compromise or consent with his Dad before he died and had supported abuses of his siblings in denial and avoiding to really hear. I felt many times sorry for Tom with his anxieties, panic attacks and a serious blackout even after attending physicians with him because it was never diagnosed as Passable Suppression. Tom had a history of two other criminal charges that were defended that he had removed from records—one with a good lawyer and the other with three good friends, two R.C.M.P.'s and one President of a company.

Today, women are quoted as saying at International Women's Day that we still have a long way to go on quality and respect as violence continues to be a serious problem and men hire a great lawyer, lie with lack of witness and the charge gets reversed with the woman the victim.

I was personally exhausted with the continuous anger and trashing of my father-in-law well after he was dead. Never did I realize this behaviour of Tom would linger until he blamed me not realizing my loyalty and attempting to help and I was the next victim. The woman also has no lawyer—the law states the public attorney will represent her. I never even had a conversation with him.

When the oldest brother died he disclosed over his last years of life, as he battled cancer, the severe abuse he had received from his father in his rearing age to his wife. The details of using a belt and much more abuse devastated his wife to the point that she was almost bedridden with sedation for the year following. Secondary disclosure has caused her long-term emotional harm. She never really understood why at this late date that something triggered in him to tell all. The only reason she could rationalize to his revelation about his exploitation was it was accepted as a disgrace until more recently. Not his fault. Research results demonstrated that boys suffer from abuse just as profoundly as girls do. It sure was kept a secret and counselling and treatment was needed before people die as the trauma it can cause but she stated maybe he was afraid that his living brothers would do something to her. She did not know

It has been said that growing distance does automatically spell disaster but can also be a part of a cycle that returns to redefine the relationship in a new form and recapture even surpass the intimacy they once had as shown in the letters early on. But it was insurpassible. I think the greatest stumbling block was the psychological hate that Tom denied for years for his Dad and was nasty to many people, lied to his kids and reversed his hate to me but always wanted recognition from his Dad.

Finance is never considered to be the main focus of marriage but it, coupled with abuse, was a double whammy. I should not have ignored the importance of it. The idea of this book is to have an interesting read and to educate women about relationships and hopefully before marriage realize finance as history and finance as essential. Know the family history before you take the leap. Know your man. A manic disposition is a genetic predisposition. In this case, it was complemented by a gifted intelligence leading to monetary success but a vulnerability to anger and rage. Temperament is an inborn basic predisposition readily recognized by parents says the therapists Tom's Mom had told me that he was the kid most like his father. In this case, traits recognized were meddlesome, anger, pushy, do not take no for an answer, and tempers are unpredictably explosive. The scars left on the hearts and souls of childhood abuse need to stop so another generation does not inherit these scars. A man that comes to terms with his past, a devoted wife should be his advocate but if he denies, it only worsens and a wife can only do so much without professional therapy.

# CHAPTER 7

## The Assault

Even as a strong individual and a nurse that had witnessed patients out of control, I was traumatized by Tom's exploding, negative remarks and his hands around my neck choking me. This was stress personified and I could feel the increased secretion of my stress hormones. Fear for my life. Fight or flight—I chose flight using validation therapy.

This could have been prevented as could three other attacks and two other criminal charges if the family secret had come forth earlier in our lives and therapy be applied to focus on the severe anger suppression he had. There always was some intermittent conflict but it never came to mind that I should need fear for my personal safety, along with my kids but immediately after he lied then denied the abuse in his family I realized therapy was necessary but refused.

He was unpredictable and would explode in a mean fury for nothing at times. The pump at the cottage when it would not prime, putting tinfoil in the garbage by mistake, wallpapering—no real reason. No one is perfect and few people remain calm and level-headed all the time but usually have some remorse. He never did. The rages excelled over the years with everyone excusing him—including me. I really never knew what would set him off or get him into a sarcastic mood but I would remove myself. Only in the last years before separation did he become physical and I had a lock put on my bedroom door.

I came from a childhood where I was always too ready to accept responsibility, make changes and it was a given. I did internalize my feelings of humiliation often as he decided to erupt—even in public. The assault had mortified me. Instead of love and romance, there had been anger and fear. Hard to work on. Embarrassed and ashamed that I did not enforce therapy especially as a professional.

He was the first significant man that made me feel things were my fault and that I was inadequate and so I tried and tried but it was probably my unawareness of his insidious abuse. He did get nicknamed "The white-haired" of the clan of his siblings. He was definitely an overachiever and I could not keep up and have some fun in life and happiness with him. Never enough. I was raised to be strong and independent. Thank God.

When I look back, it's unbelievable to me how this man was able to also con me as I tried to support and love him. The moment I surrendered my money when we were first married I was on a tight budget and had to learn to do whatever to manage to feed and dress the kids and me. I remember making a whole winter outfit out of $1.00 worth of material. "Why in the world would anybody in their right mind transfer funds that you worked hard for and sell your car?" my mother would ask. "When I die and leave you money, do not give a cent to him." my mother would also say. I ignored her wealth of information and I bought a boat and bikes for all at the cottage to have fun, trips, clothes, etc., etc. Too generous and kind was a disability to keep peace in the family.

The secret that he had been harbouring, looking back, made me realize that he was completely self-absorbed, primarily talking about himself and his gains in money. He took no interest in my achievements nor the kid's—in fact, put down teachers and failed to recognize me as a Registered Nurse.

He bragged about heavy hitters in the market. His self-aggrandizing behaviour never bothered me but it did others as I loved to entertain and got feedback I really did not need. This was probably insecurity from his younger years and that I never observed as a sign or symptom of abuse.

I realize all this exposure to Tom's negative remarks and lack of any appreciation became the norm. The last time I entertained he made a sly remark as we passed in the kitchen, "You are just showing off." He replicated the agonizing pain of his father's hostility towards him. He was never able to release his true regressed anger and finally transferred to assault. Recurring cruel words I remember were cheap shots—bitch, spoiled brat, showing off and "if you think my father behaved poorly—watch me."

Tom's mother was a sweet lady but financially controlled and abused. In fact it was sad she died before her Old Age Pension (her first cheque). She never had much money for food so on many visits I always compensated as best I could bringing steaks, pies, etc. She had nothing and at one point tried "breaking out" leaving Edgar and took a job in the city but he bullied her back. She told me it was a huge mistake to be chased back. In her last years, she was treated without medical care but medicated by her husband. I wanted to take her into my home but Tom said no—another mistake on my part. She died from a massive cerebral hemorrhage, three weeks after my request to have her taken by ambulance to the city. Her last words that I heard were, "Do not let that man (her husband) come into my room." Naivety and lack of awareness and guts can cause hurt to so many people. Someone has to stop the flow and legislation for the victims needs change.

Tom hated his father for his abusive ways but he became, in the last few years, a carbon copy of his Dad—verbally and physically abusive. Never incest that I know of because I stood up to autocratic parenting. Positive reinforcement with philosophy "children learn what they live" as hung on the kitchen wall to this day was and is my philosophy. But always contested in all my responses in the divorce decree that Tom had medical problems and was not in a clear, rational frame of mind.

The loopholes in the legal system allowed him to hire the best criminal lawyer and me the so-called specialist crown attorney for the battered wife. If there was a no-witness which is 90% of the time, the result it is said as too subjective and the wife loses. The crown attorney never even talked to me and I was not allowed in court. The legal system is not for the victim and she suffers for the rest of her life.

The laws as they stand and even give the perpetrator, my husband, the chance to lie and convince my adult children that it never happened—denial, avoidance and lies adding to the post traumatic hurt of me the victim.

We need change in the laws because as they stand it is a deterrent for the abused not to report an abuse that can even lead to serious physical hurt, murder and a lifetime of mental torment. It is now 2 ½ years and my trauma is there and agitated by my children as their father reinforced that I lied. It behooves me that a father would put his children who are raising children through these lies, hurts and trauma.

# CHAPTER 8

# My Family

The land that my paternal ancestors settled in the year 1832 was the Eastern township near Ottawa from Scotland.

The cottage they built was situated on a hill which was known for its beautiful view. It was also said that the importance of families was seen through all generations as demonstrated in the book *Yesterdays Beginning* by a cousin who wanted the story of a pioneer couple with genealogies of their eleven children.

Things were not easy as the settlers lived in whatever accommodation was available, often under canvas until a cottage of logs was erected.

Little is known of my maternal legacy at this time but Mom originated from the United States of America. Her father was a logger and they travelled from Michigan to Oregon. My mom had two sisters and two brothers that were well-educated in Catholic boarding schools.

We were not poor and not rich but comfortable because my father had a constant and secure job in the Depression. He was a Captain on the big steamships and a gentle man that gave me stability. We bought many of our products of basic food, milk, meat and some vegetables from the local farmer and grew the rest. We lived in the one full-sized home with a large kitchen, dining room, parlor and three bedrooms with indoor toiletry facilities for most of our childhood and adolescent years. We also had an outdoorsman for a father who created experiences in camping on beautiful

Lake Superior—sandy beaches for miles and great fishing while lodging in a rental wood camp or tenting.

The Great Depression had just finished when I was born. I was the middle child of three with two brothers—the younger a personality of high spirit and always spontaneous where as my older brother was methodical and organized building his life in a proactive manner. I was in between having a temperament of consistency, level-headed but did like fun and especially dancing. They went on to marry and have five children in total and to date eight grandchildren.

We had several uncles who also had farms that we would visit as very young children and would romp in the bales of hay. We were fortunate as my Dad could afford a Hudson sedan that made our life experiences enhanced with the ability to go fishing, hunting, hiking, tobogganing, many other visits that others did not have due to lack of transportation and money.

The making of maple syrup became an exciting winter experience as we tapped the trees for sap and would visit the woods once a week until we had enough to fill our large iron pot and bring it home to boil on the large wooden stove in the kitchen. It would boil down to a consistency of thick maple syrup and be sealed and put away for the coming year. So yummy on pancakes.

Our garden did produce some edibles (potatoes, carrots, rhubarb, strawberries) that did us well. The fall harvest was preserved in a cool room in the basement where we would bury them in sand. Blueberries and raspberries were also picked and canned in jars for the winter months.

My father was a superb huntsman and we had venison, duck and partridge for the year. They were frozen outdoors in the below zero weather. We were well provided for even in the winter season. Coal was our source of heat so our basement had a large bin to keep the coal.

Pets were part of growing up: two dogs and a cat. Dogs were always invited on the hunt and loved every minute of it—romping through the woods. Tom had no problem killing animals including stray cats that came to our home in the city which was so different for me. We, as kids going with

Dad an expert bushman, who would set up a fire when it came eating time and usually fresh bread and a big pot of beans cooked in salt pork. There was nothing like it, sitting on a log enjoying a hot meal with hot pork and beans in the Thermos and, of course, Mom's homemade cookies. She was not really the woods-type person as she was born and raised in the big city of Detroit. She loved Al Jolson's records and performances and theatre. My mother was a happy person for the most part of her life but the aging process took its toll.

My Dad was always a very content man thanking his "lucky stars." Mealtime was a great time for family exchanges, good wholesome food and discussions. My father always said "if your mother has taken the time to prepare a meal we owe her the courtesy to be on time and enjoy." Carrots were a big item as seen to enhance good eyesight. A good balance of schooling and recreation were seen as two essential ingredients in our lives with our chores carried out as a collaborative effort.

There were many times related to us kids about the Great Depression. Our home was on a main street a short distance from the train track that brought men in searching for work and were hungry. My Mom set up a mini food service in the back porch providing sandwiches with drinks or soup and would tell the story of how they were ravished and how we should be grateful.

In my childhood, books and stories were our great entertainment. We walked to the library with mother at least twice a week returning with three or four books. That habit remains with my younger brother and I as we love to read.

My younger brother successfully completed university as an engineer, me a Registered Nurse, and my oldest brother a supervisor at the steel plant. My eldest brother was always considered the brightest as he excelled from Grade 7 to High School and the nuns encouraged my Dad about his intelligence. My younger brother and I would tease him. Unfortunately, we lost him to M.S. early on but not before he enjoyed a great marriage with an R.N. and three delightful kids. My sister-in-law and I remain great friends to today. My younger brother travelled worldwide, married and produced two daughters but very sad to me was his male support for my husband as was other male friends. With no the victim becomes the perpetrator and.

Our grandparents meant a great deal to us. The paternal grandmom was at our home every Sunday for a great meal and the other grandma lived in the U.S. and never failed sending us kids great gifts for every special occasion and journey the long distance to see us. She was wheelchair-bound but had a great sense of humour and I loved her. Grandma Hattie.

Family was always important to me and we had a great respect for each other and shared.

Both grandmas had special skills and I learned to knit and crochet and some cooking. Family carried on being the most important focus but Tom did not have the same past so it is still questionable to me how my kids could be so hateful as their father.

# CHAPTER 9

# The Craziest Divorce Ever

The most selfish thing you can do to a family is orchestrate a divorce without keeping all saving devices. It was the morning of May 7, the start of a bright sunny day when the doorbell rang. The postman with registered mail marked Supreme Court of Canada. It could not be good but in retrospect, it was, but overwhelming and put me in a state of shock. Too much happening, retirement, assault and now divorce.

The journey of divorce should be relatively straightforward with a mature individual wanting out and discussed. At this time in our life it is really only equalization of assets especially after Tom's delusion of misplaced anger to me. A possible blessing, I needed some peace, happiness, security, definitely less work as "Katie in the Kitchen" and the other chores that complement that job, I rationalized. I was tired, a big job, a large house and cottage to maintain and the enormous grocery shopping and cooking.

But the only people to gain from divorce was Anne, Carey and money from the Incorporation as I have reconciled since the courts made it crystal clear that finances must be exact and honest and the most important part. This became the pivotal point and brutal fight of the divorce. No forthcoming correct financial statements from Tom.

In fact, I had tried on several occasions prior to the divorce to discuss our finances as I aged but with no sensitivity in fact increased anger so the missing part of the puzzle—unknown finances. Interesting enough Anne's name was always mentioned. They say you should always do what you love doing. I love resolving people's lives to live happier lives but never had an answer to "Just wait until Anne gets you" says Tom. Never did find out. In fact his negative memos to me said that.

On May 14, I went to the shared cottage at that time to enjoy a weekend with my youngest daughter and grandkids and had a great time only to find out it was a set-up for my eldest daughter to break and enter my designated (by the courts) home in the city. She removed furniture to furnish her father's new apartment and I came home to shock and disappointment in my eldest daughter. This would happen again with denial, shock and dismay. Break and entry while the divorce decree was in the courts.

In the meantime, my lawyer repeatedly attempted to establish full financial disclosure which was definitely not forthcoming. In fact, each submission of disclosure of total finances were incomplete with company omissions.

The next disappointment was my visit to my primary physician when he discussed with me a visit by my eldest daughter made to explore my incompetency. This was very upsetting and my physician realized that it was not his ethical right to disclose any information and did not but was interested in her objective. I recalled the many times as my husband was a master in cheap shots to put me down would regurgitate. "You need a psychiatrist." One of his negative moods. In fact, my doctor was proud of my competency in spite of all the family greed and lack of support.

The attempt for full financial disclosure by my defense lawyer came to a conclusion after thousands of legal costs. He said: "Nothing more can be done." He had examined the "books" of both companies and they were a "mess." I had copies of the most recent financials which were two years old but did not suggest the company had over several million dollars but evidence showed that motions had changed my shares leaving me a few hundred bucks. Again shock, disbelief and sadness entered into my life losing self-esteem.

I was a trusting soul to a husband that had two faces and two children supporting his motions which included an "estate freeze" that I evidently signed leaving them and grandkids with the major money. I did not know what an "estate freeze" was nor did I understand the difference between a common share and a deferred share and how they were divided until I consulted a Corporate Lawyer who defined my rights. My kids and husband had taken me. In fact my kids had more to gain than my husband. No wonder they were trying to find incompetency.

Naivety personified and misplaced trust. I had some learning to do and a lawyer that could help me and I was on my own. I did know I owned my share of the house and cottage but thought that I would get equalization in company shares. This issue had been raised by a friend, a lawyer that I had requested to make my will as I was getting older and I had mentioned to Tom. I questioned Tom about the company relative to the will and I had no concrete answer—only papers that were dated some 20 years ago, the inception of the first company. Again—yes, I was conned by my husband and daughters.

I did work in Community Services where over the years had given me the privilege to work with a renown Family Law Attorney who had retired. I appealed to him to help me as I explained the proceeding to date and included the role my daughters were playing and recipients as Directors of the two companies as Common Share holders. This I discovered after requesting an Incorporation lawyer to examine the companies under the Incorporation Act. How humiliating to live with a man that was screwing you and also your kids that lied that I was informed of all details of the changing condition of companies that I did not know and understand. This is illegal as I was informed I should have had my own lawyer to interpret the changing of the Incorporation and I did not. Only after months of legal analysis by special skilled lawyers did I discover this. I still labour over trying to understand this very complicated "estate freeze" law. A lesson: never sign a document without complete knowledge. The minutes were presented to the discovery process for full financial disclosure and the company minutes lacked signatures and falsification of the place.

In the midst of the divorce process as court documents were exchanged for Tom and myself, a financial statement came in the mail to the house disclosing company in the figures which was great evidence. By this time, the kids were being considered to be named on the divorce decree because of their involvement in the motions and owned the money and shares and no intention to meet to reverse in favour of their mother which was another naivety and traumatic shock for me. I raised my kids to have integrity and so the pressure carried on. I realized they were in a place to win more than Tom or myself and Tom was vulnerable with his sickness.

We went to court to demand full financial disclosure by a judge and Tom said he had a binder that he would transfer to my lawyer that would be inclusive of financials. The judge scolded him and stated that it was not fair to treat his wife as such and second a good mediator should be facilitated to allow "your wife get on with her life." Anne attempted to attend this court session but I requested she be excused leaving me very disappointed that she was there to intervene for her self another symptom of her to be a woman *not* equalization. The white binder turned out to be nil—not complete and we attempted to mediate but my lawyer said it was impossible with Tom's unbelievable hostility and attitude.

As this legal journey took place the cost was escalating into thousands of dollars for lawyers. It was not necessary as my kids could have called for a meeting and change the motions but that was not to happen. As a mother, I remained in shock and disbelief as did my lawyer. "Those kids have not lived under your roof for 26 years," said the lawyer.

After considerable consideration, my lawyer with my permission stated that we add both children to the divorce decree as they own the family money processed through motions without my legal authorization which were my rights. Almost inconceivable to me as a mother.

The next process would be "The Discovery" with the lawyers questioning the applicant (Tom) and the responder (myself) and the two kids added to the decree. The first examination for Discovery was Tom which was a day of questioning by my lawyer. Tom was nasty from time to time answered questions. Some just to hurt me like "Is your wife a Registered Nurse?" and he responded "that was before my time." Meanwhile it had paid for his food, the bed he slept in, some trips to Montebello and the promise to take over certain invoices "so he could proceed without expenses and play the stock market," etc., etc.

The whole Discovery process showed that "Articles of Amendment" were facilitated by Tom with no legals, motions or directors' votes. It was an autocratic process to have the company conform with the so-called "estate freeze" allowing me deferred shares and the daughters common shares. It was done approximately seven years prior to the divorce. About the time that the family incest was disclosed and Tom transferred his anger to me.

Through the whole Discovery, Tom was not disappointing with his arrogant, sarcastic and adversarial tones. Playing his con artist games with numerous lies. "How many vehicles did you own in '95?" questioned my lawyer.

"I can't recall."

In fact, as I re-read the notes there was really no real information because of Tom's denial and attitude, but one BIGGY—the bank statement some millions of company dollars for personal use questioned. Tom bitterly stated "She would never find out if I could have changed the address." The company financials that were posted as part of the Annual Report did not reconcile—big time.

As we journeyed along and the trio—my kids and Tom—anteed up more money for settlement recognizing in court the truth would finally out was a sign of their guilt and the legal costs would escalate and the results—fraud and charges.

The request that I made to continue to share the cottage was taken to special court with the judge favouring my request but later on I gave in because of kids. That was a mother talking not a professional making a proactive and sensible decision. It now allows grandchildren visits for Tom and I am without. A bad decision.

Leaving inherited boats and furniture behind for their enjoyment but ostracization still exists with grandchildren. Another wrong decision.

The settlement finally came but not without months and one year of extreme trauma, tremendous stress and tears. The craziest divorce for people in their golden years in their 70's that should not waste a day of the good life God gave them. Their health, wealth and a great family destroyed only to let the children win and put a wedge in the family.

# CHAPTER 10

## The Incorporation

Many family companies have destroyed family dynamics and annihilated all or partial family members of loving, traditional relationships, and in this day, grandparents as well. The "estate freeze" in this case did that with an unacceptable legal process. The process was not meant for divorce equalization but credit children, husbands and grandkids.

The induction of an incorporation or family business is usually influenced by a person that wants to go on their own and need a structure for finances although there are self-help books that supposedly provide sufficient information of a legal and practical nature to assist in understanding incorporation procedures and assist you in enabling your own corporation which Tom did and left him in a position to change by-laws through motions he created and I signed in trust. NO WOMAN should ever SIGN a document without knowledge and understanding with her own lawyer for objectivity and understanding.

Tom was not corporate responsible and only benefitted his goals not always his clients. He gave up on writing responsible reports and was mostly a verbal consultant. This was done without consent of the Directors, to my knowledge, imposing his practices and procedures. There were corporate minutes identifying me as at meetings but that was false. Certainly as I gained knowledge with the help of lawyers, it was identified that not only were made—one I signed that changed the complete status of common and deferred shares with no legal counsel—my right, and an "estate freeze" leaving the children with a lot of money and their children and me with about $800.00.

Companies that do not operate appropriately are so incredibly unjust especially in a divorce. One factor that enters is the cost of the legal expenses and 90% of the victims, especially women, cannot afford those costs.

The laws are definitely in place for the person that opens the Incorporation—regardless of what the law says and no matter what form an organization may take, the preparation of meaningful financial audited statements are vital to any enterprise and the Directors more importantly especially if a wife is a Director. The balance sheet of the corporation would indicate an on-going basis debt for which the incorporation is liable and to determine assets. It also indicates the economic health of the enterprise.

As a very naive woman in the case of the for-profit company business, I trusted and was ignorant of the differentiation between a non-profit and a for-profit organization and trusted required documents signed without questioning and responsibility. In the last months before the major assault Tom slapped my face because I enquired and asked to read a document before signing. I realized how genuinely dumb I was. I also realized this had been a planned conspiracy with the "estate freeze" because no parent/grandparent would execute a motion that could freeze money that may be needed as you grow old. Tom's frugality stood out loud and clear creating a family incorporation without legal assistance to in his favour. It was wrong and I should have been more involved and questioned in retrospect of having my own lawyer when major motions were made to change the while Incorporation and a set-up Holding Company.

My naivety and trust shows up in so many areas of our life. A lifetime of deceit and in reality to a health professional smart lady that was conned. People should just be truthful all their life and the world would be great but that is not so. (Reference "estate freeze").

# CHAPTER 11

# The Destruction of a Family

I will never ever recover because of the multiple serious acts, even illegal processes, that have transpired without transparency and executed by the process of conspiracy by my family. I recall one night, Carey called for a specific request because in the past three years a "How are you?" never happened. In the midst of the conversation, she just dropped a line or maybe a cheap shot. "That her husband's honesty and integrity was the reason she married him." Dr. Phil refers to these comments as cheap shots but I was not prepared to respond. Maybe it was her guilt.

As a team leader, committee chair Board member experienced in many non-profits, I had become accustomed to process in a proactive, logic sequence manner, information—not reactive. Relating in an empathetic way to solve problems or get further meaning. Open dialogue with me and my children is now void even tough in early years before marriage the round table was indelible and exciting to me. It certainly may have been passed down to the next generation but marriage happens—too many scheduled activities so no time for talk or building empathetic relationships. Too many couch potato habits with TVs and computers.

Marriage of your children also add a different dimension and could be a wonderful extension to a family or destructive relative to goals, attitudes, values and principles. It could have been turned around or if done proactively with good therapy and feelings of remorse.

I never could build a connection with my son-in-laws as trying to build a rapport, harmony to empathize with them. The closest I came was when my youngest divorced. Dick would call and chat like a normal give and take. A person marrying into the family becomes a very important factor as I think in retrospect. Their temperament marks are very important tendencies that direct one towards optimism and accentuating a positive communication and can make or break a family. The old saying: "a bad apple can spoil a whole bunch." I do not know my present son-in-laws except one loves prestige, status and money.

I had every opportunity and thought I was meeting their family needs as "Katie in the Kitchen," on food and fun on many weekends. Also purchaser of the food to make delightful meals especially as the family grew to five grandkids. Bikes, boats were made available to have fun. Nothing worked as I could not claim good psychological connections definitely deficits which I never understood but again did observe sarcastic remarks about my elder daughter by her husband behind her back but ignored it. None of my business, I said to myself. Tim loved the exotic world but did not to work for it. A good thing to hang his tail to daughter number one who was conspiring with her father for millions under my very face and I did not see it.

Oh, how deceptive the world can be if you believe in people while you are working your derriere off with a very responsible job, keep two big houses, clean, shop and pay for all the groceries that your head is spinning and the recipient, the son-in-law states, "He hates me." Never had a conversation with the man. In fact, prior to marriage, he overstated his worth by boasting about stocks and this great car—where? In fact, it was stressed that he would not please us with his company if the larger cottage had not been built. While building, he was provided with motel accommodation. He had free range and I again naively did nothing. This so-called man had dropped or failed University but managed to go back after marriage to finish a BA. He seemed to be okay and had a job and was anxious to have kids. The second son-in-law ended in divorce after four years. He could communicate as I built a great rapport and could chat often—a down-to-earth small time kid like me. The second husband, although a lawyer, exudes a body language to me that one would classify as distant and never a laugh shall we hear. On the other hand, no son-in-law made any attempt to connect with me to empathize and I tried with my assault and divorce. It may be a surprise but many sons-in-laws do work on extended family which is great—more people, more fun, more learning and sociability.

During my daughter's divorce, my role was to give her support which I did every weekend taking her to the cottage even shortening my vacation to be with her but there was no sense of gratitude. In fact, hostility—scapegoating on me.

My kids did not support me but played a major role in my divorce, they were "enablers to divorce for money." Company changes were obvious even identified by Tom's best friend. "Divorce but do not cheat on finances," said Ed from Australia.

My kids do not have the history I have—how we started with nothing but the memory of the proposal and the ring given at my Mom's home in the living room. It was a special moment to me. This generation believes in divorce as a cure-all and also is the generation that looks for legacy money—entitlement as said by my lawyer most recently "Cold Blood."

Another factor that I was completely inept to was Tom's friends. Eric annually made his trip to the cottage with his companion much younger than him but after his divorce encountered her. His precipitated divorce from a loyal woman who had beared him two beautiful children and several grandchildren. Bimbeau was his lady's name and as usual I treated her as most guests—lovely homemade meals, encouraging her to use the boats, etc. but little did I know she was on the hunt for a friend to latch a wealthy man. Eric was a wealthy man as was Tom that I had no idea at that time, completely naive but a million dollar cottage was definitely a statement. She said one day: "Watch your man. I have women friends that would die for him." I again was silly to believe Tom and I had come too many years—some up, some down but solid because of the family and resources we had built. It was a team effort I had thought so let it go in one ear and out the other. Another mistake. Took the high road to what I thought as a rather unintelligent woman and carried on the good mannered hostess that she certainly enjoyed taking even from time to time in my absence even using my home-cooked frozen food.

Tom also was free with advice and almost caused his other friend a second divorce as the wife discovered a transfer of a cottage to the first son of the first marriage. Again a very trustworthy woman. There is so many of us.

Marriage of 40 years did not educate me and inspire me and no doubt I was connected or not paying enough attention—I could have been a street lady at 70 years of age. Money is essential for security but I won after extensive stress, health problems and an exemplary lawyer.

# CHAPTER 12

## The Importance of Wonderful Old Friends, Cohorts, New Friends and Achievements

"In crisis, a friend is like a Brick of Gold," and volunteerism is a saver of your heart and soul to give to others.

For forty years of my life I resided in the big abominable city with its busy people, multi-tasking, tight schedule, challenging transportation, working in a position with stress personified . . . but enjoying it at the same time and giving back while implementing programs and services for the oppressed. Extremely rewarding.

However, on weekends, I had the luxury of going to the country. The diversion was almost deafening with the quiet stillness of peace, sitting on the dock observing the loons on the lake, walking in the woods, and one of my favourites—time to read not to speak of biking with my grandchildren as they grew and I got to know them as individuals.

One day a neighbour came through the screen door with a big "hello" and announced that she was scouting for Bridge players and heard I played. I was pleased to be asked as it would introduce me to unhurried people and love the challenge which I had little time for of late. She introduced herself as the lady from up the street and she hoped to form two tables of players. I, of course, said "yes" and she said, "good, we start next Wednesday and hope for weekly events," and the ladies' Lake Bridge has gone on now challenging Bridge while enjoying great company.

That is ten years ago and the game brought not only healthy competition, learning, but a sense of family sharing and caring for each other on a weekly basis.

However, this wonderful life of friends and fun was not interrupted by the family crisis of divorce and assault and my usage of the cottage. One day I opened the door to the Bridge gang and they handed me this big bag and upon opening almost in disbelief was a hand-crafted friendship quilt with 12 squares describing me as they interpreted me as a person. What a gift from such caring people that demonstrated a great labour of love and I carry on with this wonderful group in the north to date. As it hangs in my bedroom in my place every morning I awake thinking how wonderful the country folks are and the wonderful world that we live in. The square Marie created was my love for a good cup of coffee. Beth stating my flaming red hair. Dianne, my addiction to books, a loving grandma by Jane and on and on finishing with a pattern of hearts. A complete love of labour by Lonnie.

As you go through such processes of assault and divorce and are emotionally, spiritually, physically down, friends are invaluable. They, in essence, divert your sadness to happiness especially in my case where my kids supported Tom. I was anguished, hurt and beyond myself as I did not understand.

The girlfriends in the city were equally supportive, as I had known them for years, inviting me over for dinner, chatting and of course weekly Bridge.

My nursing classmates called and reminded me of my graduation that was a blast after three intense years of long hours of practice combined with academic study at the Hospital School of Nursing at that time. I had just turned 21 years of age, an RN, full of spirit, vigor and ready to challenge the world. The black band on my stiffly starched cap symbolized that "I had made it"—a Registered Nurse graduating with lifetime friends which were great support after 40 years in my time of crisis of this devastating Divorce and Assault.

I fondly remembered the Graduation Hall had beautifully decorated tables with royal blue and yellow and I was escorted by what I called "a Hunk," a young physician Henry Bernard. I had met him in Toronto and we danced the night away with me dressed in a long yellow frock with a crinoline

under garment, making the dress stand out and flowed like a rippling stream as the music played on. I felt like the belle of the ball.
I had also been awarded the honour of the Valedictorian of the Class for the graduation ceremonies which gave me a chance to voice the philosophies of my classmates (reference). I stood up and looked into the audience of parents, doctors, nurses, nuns, clergy of about 500 people and thought to myself "I cannot do this" but the words were already flowing out as I looked down at Sister Madonna of the Sacred Heart, our Director of Nurses, with a usual rigid look on her face and a posture straight as a board.

"There is in humans four fundamental incentives in life: the desire for new experience, the desire for security, the wish for recognition and the wish to help those in need." This I stated clearly in my valedictorian and "Now we go to with challenges to be met because we are women, because we are nurses, and because we are children of God." A great night was had by all and prepared us for our next experience and challenge in the wonderful world of caring. One of the speakers, Dr. Brown, stated that these women graduating will make the best mothers of the future.

So within days, I had accepted a position as a charge "Real Nurse," to quote the student nurse instructor on a medical/surgical ward with a bed capacity of 60 patients working in teams of three. It was exciting and so was the feeling of being in charge of the team, the wards. It gave me a feeling of new experience but also fearful of my own inadequacy with so many varied diagnosed patients from gastrectomies to coronary thrombosis. So much more to learn. Fortimycin the first penicillin was approved and giving 50 intramuscular injections was an easy day as well as learning intravenusclysis. Penicillin was a miracle drug as we saw many patients recuperate so quickly.

I recall one neck injury, and a friend Arnold Smit. He had been admitted on the night shift and as I took over as head nurse I realized that his neck was not immobilized in sand bags and if he moved break his neck leaving him a paraplegic so within minutes was in tongs and traction with a cervical simple fracture on my quality nursing. Very serious because any movement could cause paralysis. This case, among many, stood out in my mind because he was such a good friend and our hockey champion. A small city, people knowing each other.

Social life continued with Dr. Bernard lasting for six months and Mike White, a lawyer, entering my life with dancing and skiing on weekends. Lots of fun with no serious commitments. One of my classmates, Ali Young, and I took to some travel to Montreal to enjoy some theatre and meet two gentlemen we knew at the University, and glorious shopping in the little French stores with such exciting new fashions for two girls from a much smaller city and money. Buy, buy and buy some more. Spike high heels with bags to match. Great fun.

The train trip was another story with a dome car that attracted the keener men and women looking for activities and we sang the night away, and generally meeting new and interesting young adults. The whole year that I was 21 seemed fast and furious but extremely exciting meeting and collecting new friends that would carry on. My life always put me in a place of trust and good people.

In marriage, all the places that we moved in seven different houses in nine years were too fast and furious to nurture solid friendships. In Anitou, I did work in the hospital with two special nurses that the relationship remains the same with Christmas cards and long-distance calls. Great nurses and great women.

The friends and encounters while working at the Community Services were insurmountable and need a separate chapter. (See reference.) Twenty-seven years of growth, happiness, creating services while working with wonderful people sharing different skills that were a support group to me. I lucked out on a couple of particularly special people working in the services and has continued on. They are not only open communicative folks but are a personal asset to me—one, a Social Worker and the other a Word Processor expert.

Volunteerism was introduced into my life very early on and was a survivor for me many times. I was only six years old when my father would journey to a Native Reserve to meet the chief that would be skilled enough to be employed by my Dad's company to try and break their passive way of life. He taught me to volunteer and play with the children who were so shy and timid, I carried on being the STAR babysitter in my neighbourhood in my hometown. The odd time someone would hand me a quarter but I loved the kids—Peter, John, Bill and little Suzie—a preparation for motherhood.

Volunteer participation and involvement has helped me throughout life and in my 70's doing Meals-on-Wheels is a joy to supply nourishment with a poor oppressed sick soul. Participating as Directors on charitable boards allows me to input my many years of involvement in social needs, implementing important programs that will maybe see a person learn to read and thus a better life. The volunteer partners are also exemplary donors and partners as in the enclosure by John. (Reference)

# CHAPTER 13

## Empowerment, Education and Forgetting

Negotiation and positive communication with love are probably the most important attribute to any relationship especially marriage. To establish this function, there should be an established respect for each other and, to be empowered, able to compromise in a relaxed environment without fear and without the threat of being wrong, scolded or hit. Every person or couple should also have a budget that is real to the revenue coming in and every wife and husband should know the family financial statements.

Forgetting is very difficult for me as is denial and avoidance. I believe in working problems through to some resolution. It is history building to me and therefore what I have done, thought and felt will not vanish because of the way I have thought it through for accountability. My conscience shows. Thinking matters through before we act is proactive and brings about a person to live with integrity. This process gets rid of emotional reaction, judgement and moves toward differences in opinion thus learning from one another.

Finance is stated as the number one problem-cause of divorce in the States today. It causes pain because it results from lack of connection established for years. Emotion also shuts down. I had been shut down for sometime and withdrew about finances over the years because of the defense it caused in Tom after I went to work and I budgeted, spent and saved and it balanced our life, no financial talk. In retirement, I acknowledge finance was a question.

To keep friendships alive and marriage, I thought I did in supporting Tom by shifting jobs, going to the doctor with him attempting to diagnose his anxiety, panic attacks, supporting him in his second offense but money was a hang-up.

Finally, education of abuse and domestic violence should be more prevalent in schools, hospitals, agencies and the general media. We need to stamp out violence completely. Do not shut down, open up and remember children get married and change.

I often think that giving, caring and the desire to please taught to me as a child in nursing was a liability. I became a trusting adult and this became a burden in my case. It became an expectation from my husband, my children, meals, clothes, keeping the house and cottage in perfect condition open to entertainment at the drop of the hat. I think I was intrigued by Tom's ability to really gamble in the Stock Market but fear as well until a certain age. I had a steady job with much less so that gave me security for the family as well.

I could be as happy as I was with a nursing career from Medical Surgical to outpost hospital care, life and death experiences, psychiatric and Community Services of broad programs from seniors to the most oppressed which changes the whole community and is reference in total.

Naivety was not in my profession but in marriage and the offspring and certainly was worse by my mother. She was a strong but very ethical woman who never missed work even with the worst ulcer I have ever seen.

Back to school at 70 was intentional after the mess of my life to seek out a place that I can grow and learn.

# EPILOGUE

Until that fateful moment in my life, I had been doing reasonably well planning for my retirement doing things I never had time for realizing work had been a great part of my life in fact almost conclusive after children. Tom still would come home drunk or late and go to bed and I had accepted that part of his life.

Tom had said "He would never retire" so I took that into consideration with disappointment as the golden years are few and with health and enough money I was sure we had my RRSP and his so we could enjoy life. I was planning a trip to the Nurses Reunion as I never had time prior to now.

At first it is a total embarrassment as you meet people or friends for the first time they ask "How did it happen?" There are many caring questions but it brings the hurt back. The most dispelling is how the kids took their father's side from the beginning and that was alluded to so many times. They never were close to their father. In fact distant, as he had never learned to connect.

The enormous trust and giving in my life I have discovered were deadly for me as a wife, mother and grandmother. It was slow and silent and ending in traumatic shock. I feel I shall never be whole again.
To be a good wife and mother, I strived doing all the good things and it became expected.

I did all these things to feel loved, respected, create happiness and it really turned out to be just "Katie in the Kitchen." Women are natural nurturers but I was more than naive. My mother said repeatedly of my temperament: "It takes little to keep her happy."

The institution of marriage has transformed every part of my life and I can see it in my daughters who were happy-go-lucky with proud achievements in their life. Their communication is either moody, mute or pushy—a new temperament to me.

Tom really thrived on marriage. The emotional well-being, exemplary, psychological and physical support was dependent on marriage and me—especially early on as he lacked self-esteem and compromise—money was his security, his father's idol was also money and assets. A learned temperament but his demands and expectations were too much.

Parenting is the hardest job a mother will ever do because of the scope of human beings. All kids have unique needs as individuals and that is hard without continuous dialogue. Mothers and women are my heroes.

Edwards Brothers,Inc!
Thorofare, NJ 08086
01 December, 2010
BA2010335